Nurses Are From Heaven

Nursing Through Eyes of Faith

Christina Feist-Heilmeier, RN, MSN

Nurses Are From Heaven
Nursing Through Eyes of Faith
by Christina Feist-Heilmeier, RN, MSN

Printed in the United States of America

ISBN 978-1-60647-910-0

www.xulonpress.com

DEDICATION

This work is dedicated to you,
the nurse reading it,
in humble appreciation for all your
many, unrecognized,
random acts of Caring.

CONTENTS

ACKNOWLEDGEMENTS

This grateful heart of mine goes out to all those who have contributed to my formation over the years. First, I thank my Maker for giving me my unique set of genes, talents and traits, unlike those that ever were or ever will be. To Him be all the glory. Second, I thank my husband, for answering God's call to complement my very existence with his, in yet another unique, unduplicated entity we call our marriage. He patiently tolerates all my weaknesses and flaws and mysteriously brings out the best in me. I also thank my children for making it possible for me to know the depths of a parent's unconditional love for a child, as that which is lavished upon me from My Heavenly Father.

A great deal of credit and appreciation goes to my parents who watered, pruned, groomed, nurtured, sacrificed for, provided for, and rescued me. Although they never had to nurse me through any broken bones (klutz that I am), they surely knew when my heart needed mending. They give me a glimpse of the depths of my Father's love for me. I thank Mom for teaching me how to think and Dad for teaching me how to do. They are the best coaches, the best fans, and the best inspirations any child could ever have.

To my brothers, their wives, each of my extended family members coast to coast, and all my husband's family members, I send my appreciation for their deep, abiding love and support. You all show me that although we are many, we remain one body in a communion of living saints.

Much appreciation goes out to the vast array of contributors to my formal education: my elementary (Notre Dame) and high school

(Bethlehem Catholic) teachers, the sisters, the priests, my professors at Cedar Crest College and Walden University, all my classmates who walked the pathways of education with me as students and colleagues in my profession, my comrades from the United States Air Force and the Indian Health Service, all the students I have ever taught, and all the friends and co-workers I have known in all my many places of employment. Thank you for allowing me to know and appreciate you along my journey in life, in education, and in Nursing.

Special thanks are extended to some of the most supportive women a gal could ever want in one lifetime: Janice, Sharon, Melinda, Deb, Kim, Kelly, Annette, Ivy, Carla, Dianna, Melanie, Rose, Ruth Ann, Margaret, Julie, and each and every supportive co-worker and fellow believer. Your "go give" spirit is a real inspiration. Thanks for believing.

Profuse appreciation is sent to my proofreader, Melinda, for her help and skills, and for patiently tolerating my energy when it is over the top! Additional appreciation is sent to my daughter and tech supporter, Maria. Your artistic eye and web talents have been a blessing. To the world's best editor, my sister-in-law and sister-in-Christ, I send heartfelt appreciation. Thanks, Nancy, for sharing the talents He has given you for His glory. Your generosity and support is unmatched.

A very heart-felt apology goes to all the wonderful men in nursing who make daily praiseworthy contributions to our great profession. I am not capable of viewing Nursing through a man's eyes, nor am I hard-wired chemically or physiologically to experience or describe Nursing from a man's view. This book is slanted toward an authentically feminine view of Nursing because that is my experience and this field is predominately female. I only hope the male nurses can glean some understanding or insight about themselves or their female colleagues from reading this book. I deeply appreciate all the men who contribute to the field of Nursing. We can't do it without you.

Lastly, I would like to thank you, the reader, for even taking an interest and picking up this book. I hope and pray you are able to extract even the slightest bit of inspiration from the humble words written within. May Our Lord bless every one of you.

I give thanks to my God

every time I think of you...

...He who has begun a good work in you

will carry it through to completion,

right up to the day of Christ Jesus.

Philippians 1:3, 6

INTRODUCTION

There is more happiness

in giving than receiving.

Acts 2:35

As you can see in the dedication page, this book is dedicated to you, the nurse reader. Please accept this sincere recognition of <u>you</u> for all you do in the amazing world of Nursing. I acknowledge you for the private times you cried all the way home from work because of something that happened that day, for those difficult moments when you cried over the med cart, for the splash of blood or needle-stick you sustained, for the time the doctor demeaned you to a pulp, for how you worked all the way through your pregnancies as long as physically possible, for saving a patient's life when you went above the doctor's head to get the proper care for him, for taking time to recruit that sharp assistant or tech to your profession, and for all the times you patiently oriented that new-hire.

You deserve credit for all the cross-training you've willingly done, for your exhaustion and sweat from the one code you remember, for the time you stopped at the accident site to help the victims, for the way you daily risk your life going up in that helicopter, for being dedicated enough to cut back your hours to stay home while your children were little, for choosing creative alternatives instead of chemical restraints, for staying in the heavy snow, for helping in the tornado, or power outage, or flood, for attending your patient's funeral to support the family, and for following up on the woman after she lost her baby.

Please accept the dedication of this book to you for all the births you celebrated, the deaths you mourned, the educating you've done, the education you've pursued, the times you were a strong leader, the times you deferred to follow, the times you advocated, the times you lobbied, the prayers you have offered on behalf of others, and for all the other unspoken sacrifices you make. Be proud of yourself and accept this overdue expression of appreciation you so deserve.

The vignettes in this book are all based on true life events. Some you may recognize or relate to better than others. Some of the names have been changed or omitted to protect the privacy of individuals.

CHAPTER ONE

YOU DESERVE A MEDAL AND A MONUMENT

Take courage and be stouthearted,

all you who hope in the Lord.

Psalm 31:24

You are cordially invited to attend this virtual award ceremony for valiant nurses. You know them. You see them every day. They thrive in their profession in spite of difficult circumstances and little to no recognition. Many of their own needs remain unmet as they strive to fill those of others.

Meet Katie, RN. Katie has worked night shift for many years while undergoing multiple rounds of chemotherapy and radiation for breast cancer. She refuses to succumb to her disease, as she raises her school-aged children alongside her supportive husband.

To her we award the "Medal of Bravery." We wish Katie the very best.

Please meet Ivonne, RN, MSN, active duty Air Force with over twenty years of service. Ivonne continued in her high-level position in the midst of our current state of military affairs as she supported and encouraged her husband through his cancer treatments, debilitation, and ultimate death. Although she achieved many medals from the Air Force, we honor her with the "Medal of Extraordinary Dedication" for all of her efforts both at home and within her career.

Please meet Lana, RN. Lana is a nurse manager and just returned to work after a serious bout with thyroid cancer and radiation. She shares her new appreciation of another chance at life with her staff and finds herself a lot more appreciative of all their efforts. To Lana we award the "Medal of Life Appreciation" and we hope she continues to enjoy a full and rewarding career.

Then there is Mary, RN, MSN. Mary and her husband have five children. She is a member of the nursing faculty at a local college. Mary travels across many states several times a year to serve in the military reserves. She extends her hard work and self-sacrifice across the miles to support an exhausted staff of military peers. To her we award the "Medal of Exceptional Service."

Meet Elaine, RN, who is seventy-something, retired, and extremely active in the rescue squad. She spent a full week, night and day, giving nursing care to a well-loved clergy member from the community who was dying. She witnessed many beautiful celestial events during his dying process. To Elaine we give the "Medal of Dignity for the Dying." We hope Elaine receives special recognition from the heavens for her dedication to a man who devoted his life to the service of God and others.

Let me introduce Cecelia, RN, who was called to the ED from ICU on the birthday of one of her teen-age sons. She found herself coding an 18 year old boy on *his* birthday after an accidental over-dose of cocaine and heroine. He didn't make it. Cecelia was dazed. She called home in the middle of the night to see if her boys were safe. She muddled through the rest of her shift, numbed by what she had witnessed. We honor Cecelia with the "Medal of Strength" for her valiant efforts.

Let me introduce Maryann, RN. She is beyond the age of retirement and has a colorful cardiac and pulmonary history. She continues to supervise at a local nursing home to help her daughter raise her precious granddaughter. To her we award the "Medal of

Perseverance." We hope Maryann thrives to see this little one grow to be as fine a lady as her grandmother is.

Meet Kim, RN, owner of a nursing staffing agency. She developed her agency so her staff would receive better financial compensation and have control of their schedules to accommodate the demands of family life. She also wanted to be a resource for facilities to be able to access quality nursing staff relief. To Kim we award the "Medal of Ingenuity."

Next is Ellen, RN. As she approached her nursing retirement after a fulfilling career, she transitioned into real estate where she helps financially challenged families achieve their American dream of home ownership. To Ellen we award the "Medal of Continued Caring."

Please meet Sherri, RN. Sherri was surprised one day to find herself in an unplanned pregnancy. As an unmarried woman, she had some difficult decisions to make. She now mothers, enjoys and loves a beautiful son who has brought joy and fulfillment to her life that she never could have previously imagined. To Sherri, we award the "Medal of Life Affirmation" as she continues to grow right along with her boy!

And next, meet Teresa, RN. Teresa has multiple nursing roles in the community but managed to simultaneously care for her mother and brother who were both terminally ill with cancer as well. She coordinated her family's efforts to help them both receive the best possible care and attention in their last days. To Teresa we give the "Medal of Extraordinary Dedication."

Please meet Susan, LPN. The minute Susan's son turned 18, he joined the Marines and informed her after the fact. She spent seven months of prayerful agony while he served in Iraq. As he served there, she continued her service to her residents in her work here without skipping a beat. Even as she could have been easily over-whelmed with worry, she never missed a day of work. To Susan we award the "Medal of Persistent Commitment."

Finally, we would like to honor *you*, the reader of this book. You are honored for all *your* unrecognized, random acts of kindness in your profession as well as your family life. We grant *you* the "Medal of Uncommon Valor" for all the births you celebrated, for all the deaths you mourned, for all the times you answered the lights instead of waiting for the aid to get them, for all the times you used your sharp skills to help your patient avoid coding, for tolerating the annoying fire drills, for maintaining composure and dignity while doing even the foulest of wound treatments, for willingly accepting a difficult assignment or admission, for helping your peer through her divorce, for all the times you addressed your patients' pain, and for all the times you skipped lunch or stayed late.

You deserve this medal for all the times you worked with menstrual cramps, headaches, or other pain, for the varicose veins you are suffering with from years of running the floors, for answering the phone when you wished you hadn't, for the time you covered for the nurse who had a sudden teen-age crisis in the family, for the time you hurried to a neighbor's house in the middle of the night to help, for all the educating you have done and all the education you have pursued, for all the times you were a strong leader, for all the times you deferred to follow, for all the times you advocated, for all the times you lobbied, for all the prayers you have offered for others, and for *all* the other unspoken sacrifices you make. Be proud and accept your "Medal of Uncommon Valor!" You've earned it! Only someone from heaven itself could do the things you are doing. We hope you will continue your honorable efforts for many years to come and teach the next generation of nurses how to practice the Art of Nursing as well as you do.

In Him who is the source of my strength

I have strength for everything.

Philippians 4:13

CHAPTER TWO

EVERY NURSE HAS A CALLING

Anyone among you who aspires

to greatness must serve the rest.

Matthew 20:26

Every nurse has a special calling. Ask any nurse, and you will find she was drawn to nursing because of a desire to care, to serve, or to help. For some, the calling is early in life, and for others it may be later, even as a second or third career. All life events help a nurse to be a better nurse because every new experience gives her a new peek through someone else's glasses.

A CALLING TO SERVE

Many years ago, in a land nearby, there lived a busy little girl, only six years of age. She had "ants in her pants" as she squirmed in the church pew, hoping Sister Rita wouldn't need to correct her. She was trying so hard to have self-control, whatever that was. Sometimes she had to remind herself to sit like a lady because she was wearing her classic, plaid jumper just like all the other girls. Oh, how she struggled to concentrate on the things Father was saying. He prayed about the moment when our Lord was condemned to death, and how He willingly took up His cross. The little girl's mind wandered to the beach. She rattled her brain once again, forcing it to pay attention to the next moments being mentioned: how He fell the first time, and then met His sorrowful mother, and how a man named Simon helped Him carry that heavy cross.

She struggled to understand why everyone needed to think about these things, yet felt a great inner peace as she participated. Then, a woman named Veronica wiped His face, just before He fell the second time. Other women grieved nearby, too. He took a moment to speak to them. After sustaining yet another fall, He was stripped of His garments and nailed to the cross He had been carrying. The little girl shuddered to think of the tremendous suffering endured by this Man. "What does it all mean? How could I help?" she wondered. Father continued to pray about the cross being raised up, where our Dear Lord continued to suffer before He finally died. His body was taken down and laid in the tomb. But this is not the end. His story doesn't stop here at a tomb, just as our story never ends. The good news is that He was not swallowed up in death and neither are we. He rose and lives, even now, just as we can!

Five years later, the same maturing girl sat in another class. She was captivated by Sister Denise's words. Sister spoke of her own calling to a life of service as a sister and teacher of children and she explained how her boyfriend wept when she shared with him that God was calling her to the sisterhood. The girl wondered what God was calling her to be when she grew up. When she went home that day, she asked her mother, "Mom, I was thinking about being a nurse because I know I could help people and still be able to make a living. What do you think?" Her mother answered, "I think that would be just great."

Ten years later, the young woman officially embraced her profession after completing her initial studies. She looked to the One who showed her the way of His cross, and gave her the strength she needed to proceed in her work. She embarked on her journey into the colorful, variegated world of Nursing, never regretting her decision.

Today, the seasoned nurse still looks to Him, her source of refuge, for continued strength and guidance- as a nurse, as a wife, as a mother, and as a daughter. She waits for the day when her children approach her with their dreams. She prays for Him to guide them in their decisions and she waits, ready to respond, "I think that would be just great!" when that special day comes.

AN INTERNATIONAL MIND IS NURTURED

Having been deeply committed to my vocation as a nurse since an early age, I began to wonder what influences contributed to that decision. Maybe it was how my mind was being stretched across the globe by my teachers. All through grade school my teachers encouraged the students to pray for all the special needs of those we knew. They reminded us of the soldiers in Vietnam and all the people suffering there. They taught us about a very special woman in India. Her name was Mother Teresa and she worked with those who were dying in the streets of Calcutta. We prayed for her and her sisters.

One day, our class was interrupted by a request over the loud speaker, "Please take a moment to say a prayer for a church member who passed away today." I stopped to pray for the anonymous person and his family. It was several hours later that I found out it was my own grandfather that we had prayed for that afternoon. He left my grandmother widowed with two teens.

On another occasion, I sat mesmerized, as Sister Denise shared about her dearest friend who chose to work with the lepers in Africa. She put herself at risk for contracting the disease herself, as treatment was not widely available at that time. I was fascinated by the selflessness and devotion of this mysterious woman in Africa and wondered if I could ever be that brave myself. I hoped someday I could be. I took my studies seriously, for each lesson brought me one footstep closer to my vision. I thought, "Maybe I could have *that* kind of dedication working as a nurse."

Even as a teen, the vision was already a reality in my mind. I began working as a nursing assistant the minute I turned sixteen, enthusiastically. I finally arrived in the healthcare arena. I was finally taking care of patients. When did you finally arrive at your first patient's bedside? What led you to your calling?

INSPIRATIONS FROM BRAZIL

I spent the summer after I became a nurse aid in Brazil as an exchange student, which only further confirmed the calling. My inquisitive eyes devoured the sites all over the city and within the home where I was a welcomed guest. It was just like the foreign scenes Sister Denise had described, as my heart was pierced with the shocking sights. A woman was sitting on a sheet on the sidewalk with several small children. Her hands were in the air as she asked for money to feed her children. Another man sat yards way from her. He was inhaling a powdered drug from an inflated brown paper bag he was holding. Dogs with mange roamed the streets. A man with elephantiasis struggled to move his heavy legs to walk. The saddest sight of all was the young children rummaging around in the massive garbage heaps acres long. By far the most puzzling sight was that of all the others, seemingly oblivious to these scenes I was noticing. They went about their daily lives, blinded to the needy before them.

I ask you how can God survive

in a man who has enough

of this world's goods yet closes his heart

to his brother when he sees him in need.

1 John 3:17

At night, through the window near my bed, I could hear the children crying in the slum behind the house. They cried from hunger, disease, neglect. I thought of the needy children in my own country and realized that I did not have the resources to help them there either. All I had the ability to do was to try to make a difference day by day, one person at a time, wherever I found myself. At age sixteen, I already knew I could only help in the big picture of humanity by acting in my own local sphere of influence.

Jesus created the connections between

saints when he hosted the first communion,

the Last Supper.

People of faith have been concerned with the broad scope of humanity since the inception of the Great Commission, 2000 years ago. They were already connected to the other people of faith everywhere, even us, the people of their future. They are connected to all believers through the communion of the saints of the past, present, and future. Believers do not need satellites and technology to stay connected as we see today. Jesus created the connections between saints when he hosted the first communion service, the Last Supper. How ironic that the first communion was labeled the Last Supper. Maybe it could have been better named as the "First Supper," since the meal continues to be celebrated today in Christian churches of all denominations universally.

Because the loaf of bread is one,

we, many though we are, are one body,

for we all partake of one loaf.

1 Corinthians 10:17

THE BREAD IS LIFTED UP

People were scattered in pews throughout the church nestled in the town of Bethlehem, PA. A woman was there meditating on the meaning of communion. The bread was lifted higher to offer thanks and for everyone to see. Suddenly, the woman was thrust into a serene and peaceful location, outside of time and space. She knew she was at the very table of the Lord, surrounded by his apostles. It was the night before he died. Not a word was spoken as she and the men reverently contemplated the Bread, now whole, but soon to be broken. The silent yet undeniable message that reached every heart there was, "This is all that matters." She wondered what this message meant. Could it be that the whole message of salvation and the cross is represented therein?

BREAD IN EMMAUS

When He had seated himself with them to eat,
He took bread, pronounced the blessing, then broke the bread and began to distribute it to them.
With that, their eyes were opened and they recognized Him; whereupon He vanished from their sight.
They said to one another,
"Were not our hearts burning inside us as He talked to us on the road and explained the Scriptures to us?"

Luke 24:30-32

CHAPTER THREE

WHERE HAS ALL
THE CARING GONE?

Nobody cares how much you know

until they know how much you care.

John Cassis [1]

Only recently has Nursing been recognized as an occupation of professional status. Therefore, much of formal nursing theory is only recent in history. Who ever thinks to connect Biblical principles to modern nursing theory? Even though the Art of Nursing has been practiced since the dawn of human existence when women assisted in childbirth and infant care, there are very few who take our current view of connectedness to the Creator, planet earth, and the universe across the portals of time to those roadways leading us to the Biblical centuries and millenniums that preceded us. (Even fewer nurse theorists conceive of a connectedness to the centuries and millenniums which will follow us.) Dare we consider ourselves contemporaries of those who have already been or those who are yet to come? Who are the great women who have come before us? Are they Florence Nightingale and Mother Teresa or the Biblical women even further back like Ruth, Anne, Esther, the sisters of Lazarus, and Mary the Mother of Jesus?

In His ministry, Jesus gave us many examples of how to treat the poor, the sick, the widows, the orphans, and the disenfranchised. He demonstrated great compassion, pity, and sympathy.

At the sight of the crowd, his heart

was moved with pity.

They were lying prostrate from exhaustion,

like sheep without a shepherd.

Matthew 9:36

CARING: THE ONLY FOUNDATION

We hope that the majority of nurses make Caring the foundation of their philosophy on Nursing. Nursing is the art and science of promoting the total health of individuals or groups. Total health is the optimal spiritual, mental, and physical well-being possible for a person or a population. Nursing practice is accomplished by preventing or deterring disease, by contributing to health and wellness maintenance, by educating or leading those who do these activities, or by teaching those who will do them. The science of nursing practice involves the intelligence, knowledge, and skills needed to ensure competency in all types of nursing duties. The art of nursing practice involves the manner in which the duties are accomplished. Primarily, all nursing practices and activities must demonstrate Caring towards the recipients. The clients (as patient, family member or student) receive their care and education in a dignified and compassionate manner with all rights and diversities being treated with utmost respect.

We hope that the majority of nurses

make Caring the foundation of

their philosophy on Nursing.

The patient is the recipient who benefits from the work and Caring of the nurse. The client can be an inpatient, outpatient, student, trainee, subordinate, child, or random member of the community. The nurse carries her caring, intellectual, and interpersonal expertise into all facets of her life. This expertise is not confined to the workplace, but extends into all relationships, especially those with her loved ones and community members.

The environment serves either to promote or deter the nurse's total health promotion process. The environment promotes the process by making collaboration with other people and resources possible in order to help the client and to promote total health, Caring, healing, and education. Unfortunately, the environment can serve as a deterrent to wellness of individuals through the compromises and insults directed at them from outside sources including people, activities, communicable disease, pollutants, natural disasters, and intentional harm.

Labor to keep in our breast that little

spark of celestial fire called conscience.

George Washington [2]

When we practice Nursing for any length of time, we are exposed to the diverse roles nurses can play in various nursing arenas: medical/surgical, obstetrics, drug rehabilitation, pediatrics, critical care areas, home health, community nursing, and gerontology just to name a few. The list is endless. The single element common to every area of nursing is Caring. Caring is responsible for many nurses' original commitment to Nursing.

Many nursing theorists have thoughts on Caring. Two theorists, Boyken and Schoenhofer, emphasize that the nurse weave a caring, fond approach to her patients throughout the nursing care provided. The theory is called the *Nursing as Caring Theory*. The theory does not negate the need for knowledge of other scientific and psycho-social disciplines also required to perform Nursing. This theory simply puts the Caring first and above all else. Caring Theory assumes that because people are human, they are caring. Caring makes them whole and enhances the value of those they serve. Caring Theory also assumes that Nursing is a discipline as well as a profession. These theorists believe Caring Theory applies widely throughout the profession, even to nursing administration, advanced practice nursing, nursing education, and research and development.[3]

For nurses, sometimes Caring is a decision and not always an easy one. This reality applies to our patients, our spouses, our children, and our co-workers. People need to be good to each other. Every new patient encounter is a new decision of our free will to either de-personalize and objectify the person, or to embrace the opportunity to truly care for and with them.[4] Caring behaviors are healthy and therapeutic for both patient and nurse. Historically, such behaviors are admired all through the Old and New Testaments of the Bible. For example, David soothed the anxieties and troubled mind of King Saul and Ruth dedicated herself entirely to the well-being of her mother-in-law. The Good Samaritan stopped to nurse a complete stranger, and the gravid Mary, the mother of Jesus, hurried to help her older, expecting cousin, Elizabeth, in her pregnancy. Many of these ideals were foundational in the nursing philosophy of Florence Nightingale, but have lost their power and popularity over time. In Nightingale's writings, she makes it undeniably clear that her motivation to caring and efficient nursing practice resulted from her deep faith.

Caring is a decision.

DYING WITH DIGNITY

I once cared for a man who, in his dying days, was repulsive to most of the nursing staff. Although he had been a long-term resident for many years and was well-known to all, there were many staff members who were reluctant to care for him because of various drainages and foul odors that issued from him. The resident was a well-educated gentleman. He had suffered a motor-vehicle accident when he was a young man and lived the rest of his life as a quadriplegic. After many years of living in this state, he was actively dying. There was one dear nurse aid named Mo who was willing to enter this alert and oriented patient's room with me and care for him in the manner he deserved: with dignity.

Mo is from Africa. He is a very caring individual and wins the hearts of the residents easily by consistent Caring and the individualized attention he provides. We entered the patient's room together, determined to make a difference. We made creative art with different ostomy supplies to collect the drainage issuing from his suprapubic stoma and fistulas, and to cut down on the odor. We cleansed him thoroughly and did every comfort measure imaginable. We tried to make pleasant and reassuring conversation with the patient while guarding our facial expressions so as not to portray disgust.

Mo and I non-verbally recognized the collective choice we made in our hearts to look past the ugly and instead find something beautiful and human there. Even though we both obviously were from differing faith and cultural backgrounds, and the patient from yet another, the universal Caring surpassed all these differences. I know, without a doubt, that this patient appreciated all we did and would have done the same for either of us if circumstances were reversed. The Caring Theory assumes that others will care back, too, because we all share a mutual humanity and we are all called to care. [5] Mo and I could sense that the Caring was reciprocal.

There once was a man centuries ago who also was liberated when he chose to look past the ugly to find something beautiful and human in people. His name was Francis, from the town of Assisi in Italy. He was the son of a wealthy merchant who gave up everything to pursue God as his sole purpose in life.

Francis went about tending the lepers whom he formerly found repulsive. Once Francis got past the ugly and grotesque to finally love the creature of God inside, he was liberated. He gently witnessed to the sick through his prayerful actions. The sick were able to experience the Gospel with action instead of words. Francis would say that he preached all day long and only sometimes he used words.

The Prayer of Saint Francis

Lord, make me an instrument of Your peace;
Where there is hatred let me sow seeds of love;
Where there is discord, let me sow seeds of union;
Where there is doubt, let me sow seeds of faith;
Where there is despair, let me sow seeds of hope;
Where there is darkness, let me sow seeds of light;
And where there is sadness, let me sow seeds of joy.

Oh Divine Master, grant that I may not so much seek
To be consoled as to console You in others;
To be loved, as to love You in others;
For it is in giving that we receive.
It is in pardoning that we are pardoned,
And it is in dying as a seed to our selfishness
That we are born to eternal life. [6]

CARING AS HEALING

Nursing as Caring is socially significant in that the caring nurse promotes a less anxious patient and a more favorable clinical outcome due to increased education, reassurance, and patient compliance.[7] For example, an anxious and aggressive patient who is not cooperating might respond better to the nurse he recognizes and trusts as a caring one. This psycho-social and clinical impact on patients overall is very positive when nurses are determined to exercise Caring. The actual benefits of Caring expand from single instances to the broader, overall picture of patient outcomes. For example, the same caring nurse who was able to calm the agitated patient might be the perfect nurse to facilitate this patient's discharge when the time comes to ensure compliance with all instructions as well as the plan for care at home. The specific Caring expands to the broader caring effect.

Practice is transformed

when we decide to choose to care.

Nursing as Caring Theory is practical and useful in all areas of nursing including research and education. [8] When applied appropriately, the potential for improved patient outcomes is limitless. We can easily say that Caring is universal. It spans itself across every area of Nursing and across all cultures. There are more similarities than differences when one speaks the language of Caring. Practice is transformed when we decide to choose to care.

Aside from the clinical examples, Caring in research can be practical because nurse researchers can demonstrate Caring as they collect the data from the subjects they are studying. These subjects can be other nurses, as in a study of nurse retention, or they can also be patients, as in clinical interviews. In one hospital, hundreds of patients were interviewed in order to change the culture of a hospital to a more caring one. Information was collected, ideas were planned and implemented, and the hospital's culture was changed. [9]

CARING IN EDUCATION

Caring in education is very appropriate and effective. A caring instructor can convey the information in a nursing course far more easily and effectively to students than a professor that is cold and sterile. Picture a group of clinical students. Certain clinical groups with caring, animated instructors who interact readily with the students do very well. Such caring professors take the opportunity to discover the treasure within each wide-eyed student. A professor needs to be a caring, passionate sales-person of the information she conveys. She inspires the students to "catch" the concepts and ideas taught which hopefully will translate later into competent nursing practice with Caring woven throughout.

Caring professors take the opportunity

to discover the treasure within

each wide-eyed student.

CARING ORGANIZATIONS

In keeping with the fact that people are the greatest resource in any facility, the collective wisdom and experiences of employees are especially valuable sources of information to apply toward solutions for Caring. The most practical and effective way to implement a plan for improvement in Caring in a long-term care setting is to conduct extensive interviews of residents, families, and staff. The interviews could include information from verbal and survey encounters and can be categorized, compiled, and studied to be presented to employees. The kudos from the studies could be shared and emphasized. The areas needing improvement can be addressed by a team of enthusiastic employees willing to brainstorm a plan and apply a strategy for enhancing Caring. This same team can implement the strategy by educating and providing ideas and resources to the staff. After a period of time, follow-up surveys and interviews can be taken to evaluate the plan's effectiveness. Then the process can continue, perpetually generating improvements in Caring and moving the patient care, staff, and overall facility ever forward.

People are the greatest resource in any facility.

Caring was conceived simultaneously with the inception of Nursing historically, and continues to play a significant role in

Nursing today. We must remind ourselves that Caring doesn't have to take extra time or effort. It is an intentional act of the will woven into our everyday activity. [10]

THE THEORY OF HUMAN CARING

Another contemporary nursing theorist, Jean Watson, has taken a deep look at Caring and written extensively about it. She developed a *Theory on Human Caring* which is widely accepted in the greater nursing community. Regarding the caring philosophy, Watson recognizes that there is a need for a meaningful philosophy on the nature of nursing practice. She views Nursing both as a science and an art. According to Watson, being an artist is part of a nurse's role in caring for patients and their families. She illustrates the artistic domain of nursing in what she calls her transpersonal caring-healing modalities, which include providing comfort measures, alleviating pain, stress, and suffering, and promoting well-being and healing. [11]

Very few contemporary nurse philosophers attempt to connect older, Biblically-based principles to modern Nursing and theory. Why do so few nurse theorists take their view of connectedness to a Creator, the planet earth, nature, and the universe across the portals of time to the Biblical millennia and centuries that preceded us? This concept of Caring is much older than the nursing profession itself. One of Watson's predecessors, Florence Nightingale, has also written extensively on this topic, but from a Biblical, faith-based perspective. Although these two women find themselves perched on different sections of the timeline, many of their ideas are complementary with several congruent principles noted in both their philosophies and works.

SIMILAR CARING PHILOSOPHIES

Nightingale's caring philosophy is demonstrated in her examination of Christ's identification with the poorest, weakest members of society. She wrote "I don't think any words have had a fuller possession of my mind through life than Christ's putting himself in the place of the sick, the infirm, the prisoner—and the extension which the Roman Catholic Church (especially) gave to these words, as if it were *God* putting Himself in the place of the leper, the cripple and so forth, telling us that we see Him in them. Because it is so true." [12] Nightingale saw caring for any patient as if she were caring for God Himself. Like Nightingale, if a nurse today believes that she is caring for a loving God as she cares for her patient, there may be greater motivation there to care even more.

Both Watson and Nightingale promote the idea of the nurse's investment of self by choice, intentionally, as an act of the will. Watson promotes a humanistic, altruistic value system which includes faith and hope. She wants nurses to be practicing loving kindness, making themselves authentically present, enabling and sustaining a deep belief system which includes the self and the one being cared for. [13]

In her writings, Nightingale shows that her deep faith is what motivated her to caring and efficient practice. She invested herself by choice, as an act of her free will. Simply put, she felt called to serve. She identified with Mary in the Gospel of Luke and responded as Mary did, "Behold the handmaid of the Lord; be it done unto me according to Thy word." (Luke 1:38). Florence answered her calling. For her, Nursing was a vocation - much, much more than a mere job. [14]

Florence answered her calling.

For her, Nursing was a vocation.

There is another notable similarity between Watson and Nightingale. Both view Caring as all-encompassing. Watson writes that the goal of the transpersonal caring relationship involves protecting, enhancing, and preserving the person's dignity, humanity, wholeness, and inner harmony. [15] Nightingale also sees Caring as all-encompassing. She once wrote, "When a pauper becomes ill, he ceases to be a pauper and becomes a brother to the best of us and as a brother he should be cared for." She wanted to see quality care for all, not just a system of good care for those who could afford it, with whatever charity provided for the rest.[16] Both Watson and Nightingale elude that Caring requires integrating beliefs into all areas of life and practice.

Watson and Nightingale elude that Caring

requires integrating beliefs into

all areas of life and practice.

Another area of similarity between Nightingale and Watson involves nature. Both women adoringly examine the attributes of nature and the universe to fuel and sustain their ability to care. Creation gives them a capacity to remain in wonderment throughout the caring process. Watson believes in creating a healing environment, both physically and non-physically. She describes the healing environment as a subtle environment of energy and consciousness, where wholeness, beauty, comfort, dignity, and peace are all given potential. She emphasizes the importance of making the patient's room a soothing, healing, and sacred place. [17]

Nightingale found many delights in nature, which she wrote about in her letters to others. She mused on the soap bubble and thought how good God was when He invented water and made man invent soap. She felt each bubble is delightful to the eye because each shows all the beautiful colors in the world.[18] She also had a special fondness for birds. Early in life she told a cousin, "… nothing makes my heart thrill like the voice of birds, much more than the human voice. It is the angels calling us with their songs." [19] Nightingale hinted that even non-human species share in prayer and praise. She was fond of King David's Psalms in the Old Testament which often show animals, mountains and rivers praising God. She felt that birds whisper their prayers to God at dawn each day. [20]

Nightingale hinted that even non-human species

share in prayer and praise.[20]

Nightingale was a systems thinker, which follows logically from her belief in a God of law, who made everything and is an orderly God. Her approach to healthcare was holistic. She consistently stressed health promotion and disease prevention. She felt the foundations for a good, public health system included decent housing, clean water and clean air, good nutrition, safe childbirth, and good child care. Similarly, her definition of Nursing includes well child care, as in a nanny or a mother. Her system promoted caring home visits by doctors and nurses with hospitals used only as a last resort, because she saw them as dangerous.[21] She understood the word "nosocomial" before it was ever invented.

A PRACTICAL APPLICATION OF THEORY

The nurse must be careful

enough to keep on caring.

Once a contemporary nurse looks at the similar ideals of Watson and Nightingale, she might ask, "How can their ideas help me in my everyday work?" As the nurse persists in hands-on patient care or shifts from the bedside to management, teaching, or administration, she must be careful enough to keep on caring. Many hardened hearts develop over time in all areas of nursing: staff nurses, nurse managers, faculty members, and nurse administrators. As Father Time puts more and more distance between the nurse leaders and the patient, the Caring often seems to diminish as they get swallowed up into bureaucracy.

Caring must be a constant and continuous decision for a nurse, whether as a new graduate at the bedside, an experienced clinician, an experienced educator, or a director of nurses. Nurses cannot allow the Caring they give to be affected by the surrounding circumstances of the moment - they must strive to care in every moment of practice. The decision to care consistently is not only beneficial to the patients and their families, but actually is therapeutic for the nurse. Caring contributes to the expansion of the nurse's own actualization and is beneficial for both the cared-for as well as the caregiver. [22]

Nurses cannot allow their Caring

to be affected by the surrounding circumstances

of the moment - they must strive

to care in every moment of practice.

Staff nurses are wise to be on guard against insults which assault their caring abilities, such as productivity and legal concerns in practice. Naturally these topics are important, but their effects need not limit Caring. Nurse educators must forewarn their students about the moments of disillusionment they will encounter when they do not *feel* like caring. Nurse administrators must remember that this same disillusionment affects their subordinates. As peers, nurses need to help their colleagues through difficult situations by early identification and prompt, supportive action. In many cases such awareness and support will result in keeping an employee onboard, or keeping a competent individual in Nursing altogether. Regardless of the particular job description, nurses at all levels need to know that Caring is a decision every moment of the day. Developing this mental and heart-directed skill can help keep nurses from fleeing to other professions.

Regardless of the particular job description,

nurses at all levels need to know that

Caring is a decision every moment of the day.

CARING EVERY DAY AND EVERYWHERE

May Christ dwell in your hearts through faith,

and may charity be the root and

foundation of your life.

Ephesians 3:17

As Watson and Nightingale suggest, nurses' caring, spiritual side need not be compartmentalized to Sunday mornings. Both experts elude that it is better to integrate Caring, holistically, into all areas of life including work, family, marriage, education, thoughts, choices, actions and even sexuality. Caring belongs in each of these aspects of life as an integral factor. God knows more about these areas than mankind does, so why not seek caring strength from the Ultimate Source of Caring? Faith has a huge role in nurses' motivation to practice caring behaviors at work and in the decision to both enter and remain in Nursing. As was true with Nightingale, if a nurse believes she is caring for a loving God as she is caring for her patients, there might be greater motivation to care even more. If a nurse routinely seeks refreshment and renewal for continuing on in her caring works from that same Source of Caring, the Caring is abundant and limitless.

When a nurse prays for strength

to care more, she gets it.

To continue caring is a decision. When a nurse prays for strength to care more, she gets it. The prayer is always answered. Some nurses jump from place to place for employment, looking for the greenest grasses. They will never find the perfect pasture because the satisfaction is not from the outside in, but from the inside out. There are many studies available which prove the benefits of faith in healing, recuperation, and patient outcomes. Many studies support the idea that faith and prayer drastically enhance healing. All the more that faith should be used to help maintain health and well-being of the nurses caring for these recuperating patients. Even Nightingale recommends that nurses "Go to God's infirmary and rest awhile."[23]

Go to God's infirmary and rest a while.

Florence Nightingale [23]

STAY ON THE RIGHT TRACK

When deeply studying Caring Theory, the thinking can become very ethereal and intangible. Sometimes, the heavy thinkers and philosophers get distracted by the created, shifting the focus from the Creator. If the earth and the planets and the universe and all the energies and principles of physics are so inter-connected with mankind, why not put our attention on the One who put humans and these wonders here in the first place? The One who created these is the First Carer, the First Being to care, and the First Causer to make an effect of Caring.

This same One has gifted mankind with an intelligence to share in the creative process of invention. Just as Nightingale honored the Creator for having man invent soap, [24] men and women too, can honor the Creator for helping invent the electron microscope, satellites, computers and the advanced telescopes. These inventions allow mankind to explore the depths of the microcosm and the macrocosm as if uncovering the depths of the Creator Himself. They permit man to travel deeply into the cell, molecule, atom, ocean depths, and to the furthest outreaches of space and time. As a result, the nurse can grow to appreciate His handiwork even more. The Creator's works become a never-ending Christmas morning, the uncovering of one gift of creation after another. God strategically has allowed mankind to invent such tools, so his handiwork is more deeply appreciated. Just as He saw that his handiwork was good in the book of Genesis of the Bible, so too, mankind can see human inventions are good. The intelligence is used, in Caring, to create things for the benefit of all.

If nurses view a patient or a loved one as yet another aspect of the Creator's handiwork, they will see each is also an endless gift. Each, like space and time, has limitless depths and dimensions that only the Creator completely understands. He allows the nurse to uncover and appreciate each unique individual and all the many blessings each brings to this earth. He allows mankind to care for and love others as their Originator does.

If nurses view a patient or a loved one as yet

another aspect of the Creator's handiwork,

they will see that each is also an endless gift.

With these ideals in the forefront of the nurse's mind and heart, Caring becomes much easier to do. Both nurse and patient receive therapeutic benefit. Oh, that every nurse would commit to strive to be at peace and totally present, even listening to what the person does not say in words! Oh that the little whispers and inklings from the patient would no longer be sacrificed at the altar of tension and productivity, but heard and addressed by the nurse who is careful enough to keep caring!

Oh, that the little whispers and inklings from the patient

would no longer be sacrificed at the altar of tension and

productivity, but heard and addressed by the nurse

who is careful enough to keep caring!

FAITH IS THE ROOT OF CARING

In choosing my profession of Nursing, my core values and beliefs played an integral role. I knew I wanted to be a nurse by age eleven, as a wonderful nun fostered a love of God and love for others in her sixth graders. I took my calling and vocation as seriously as she did hers. It was our choice to do as He willed. The core values in the mix include integrity, fairness, morality, respect for God and others, and love for God and others. Many nurses I have known that grew up in the 1950s, 1960s, and the 1970s have similar views of their callings, much like one of our exemplary leaders in Nursing such as Margretta Madden Styles. Margretta "dedicated her life both to God and to the profession of nursing." [25] How many colleagues today have a spiritual connection in their vocation and career? How free are we to even entertain these ideas? Often a concern for political correctness prevents a nurse from mentioning her career's faith connection.

Florence Nightingale wasn't afraid to say she saw God in every man. She knew we can view God both vertically (toward heaven) and horizontally (in others). Our core values, like Nightingale's, are imbued in our behavior within our professional and personal lives including family, parenting, marriage, leadership, teaching, and worship.

Florence Nightingale wasn't afraid

to say she saw God in every man.

A LABOR OF LOVE

Waking to a gray and misty morning, the mountain tops peaked in and out of the fog. A typical Southeast Alaska morning it was, but a very atypical day it would become for me, the new nurse. Pausing for a moment to offer a little prayer, a great and warm consolation overwhelmed me. Puzzled, I continued on my way to labor and delivery where I was met with a tremendous challenge. A beautiful Tlingit woman, very high with child, had only recently received the news that her baby was no longer alive. She remembered well her baby's gentle kicks which suddenly ceased two days earlier. We were faced with the difficult task together of inducing labor to deliver her lifeless, precious baby. I was overwhelmed with the challenge and wondered if I could possibly function well for this patient.

It suddenly occurred to me exactly why

I had received such a warm, surprise

41

consolation earlier that morning!

It gave me the courage to proceed

in this tragic task.

Carole trembled as I prepared the solution that would soon start her labor pains. I asked her if she would like to pray before we begin. She agreed as we bowed our heads saying, "Lord, we don't know why things happen the way they do sometimes, but we have a very difficult thing to do here today and we ask you to please help us. Amen." It suddenly occurred to me exactly why I had received such a warm, surprise consolation earlier that morning! It gave me the courage to proceed in this tragic task.

Surprisingly, Carole had minimal discomfort throughout her labor and the process seemed expedited by heaven itself. Her labor progressed until her little girl was born later that morning. I cleansed and swaddled the babe, and placed her in her mother's arms. Tears filled our eyes as we began to mourn her loss. We spent most of the day bonding with the baby and grieving her loss.

We cannot give on the outside what

we do not have on the inside.

Mother Teresa of Calcutta

Carole's grief lessened over time. I saw her years later in the heart of Sitka as she called to me exclaiming, "We had a healthy baby and I'm very happily married to his Daddy!" I could see it was very important to her that I hear the good news. I shared in her joy as I peered up at the glorious mountains, offering a little prayer of thanks to the One who gives life, the One who takes life, the One who consoles, the One in whom we trust.

LABOR REVEALS A LOT

There have been many other laboring women I have worked with over the years. When a nurse spends hours with a woman in the rhythm of her labor, she learns many intimate details about the patient's life. If the spouse or mate is present, the nurse can gain a rather accurate assessment of the condition of the marriage or relationship. She can easily measure the supportiveness and dedication of the spouse, especially when he remains that way even under the stress of labor. The nurse can learn all about prior pregnancies, children, marriages, education levels, religious preferences, in-laws, etc. A critically-thinking labor nurse is able to figure out early in the labor process how to best serve the patient throughout her labor and delivery. These activities include giving emotional support, implementing pain management, meeting educational needs, promoting health of mother and baby, and communicating and advocating for the patient and baby to the obstetrician.

When a nurse spends hours with a woman

in the rhythm of her labor, she learns many

intimate details about the patient's life.

A TANGIBLE EXAMPLE OF CARING

I was with one particular woman who was laboring one day. She had a history of a prior cesarean section with her first baby and it was of paramount importance to her to deliver this baby vaginally. Her process in her estimation would be a total failure to her if she didn't. After pushing for a couple of hours, she started to develop a low fever because the membranes had been ruptured for some time. I knew the baby would start to get tachycardic soon and show signs of stress. I approached the doctor and asked her to please give us just 15 more minutes to push before calling a section. She agreed, reluctantly.

I explained to the patient she needed to

reach deep down inside herself

for a new surge of strength and power.

As I approached the patient, I explained to her she needed to reach deep down inside herself for a new surge of strength and power. She had the desire, but she was tired. I convinced her that enough power was there to do it. (I would not have advocated this for every patient, but this was important for her and the mother's psychological benefit outweighed the risk to the baby.) Labor nurses know that often the greatest power in labor comes from between the ears, not from the uterus. Sure enough, the healthy baby was delivered 14 minutes later with great apgars. Even the doctor was delighted.

Labor nurses know that often the greatest

power in labor comes from between the ears,

not from the uterus.

I have grown to notice an interesting phenomenon over the years of watching labor nurses: some are so able to put their patients at ease and cooperate with the rhythm of nature that certain nurses seem to yield fewer cesarean sections. One assumption I made within this scenario was that I was the healthcare person that knew this patient <u>best</u> in the whole hospital. I knew her better than the physician did. I had to picture the patient's vantage point, the doctor's vantage point, and artfully craft the best process for the patient even though the physician had the ultimate word.

LEARN FROM THY PATIENT, NURSE

Nurses have a great deal to learn from their patients when they choose to notice. The inspirational stories from patients are countless. I once received one of those unbelievable e-mails describing a premature baby overcoming the odds. Much to my surprise, with research, I was able to reach David and Diana Blessing in Texas to confirm the information is true.

THE SMELL OF RAIN

A cold, March wind danced around the dead of night in Dallas as the doctor walked into the room of Diana Blessing. Still groggy from surgery, her husband, David, held her hand as they braced themselves for the latest news. That afternoon of March 10, 1991, complications had forced Diana, only 24 weeks pregnant, to undergo an emergency cesarean section to deliver the couple's new daughter, Danae Lu Blessing. At 12 inches long and weighing only one pound nine ounces, they already knew she was perilously premature. Still, the doctor's soft words dropped like a bomb. "I don't think she is going to make it," he said, as kindly as he could. "There is only a ten percent chance she will live through the night, and even then, if by some slim chance she does make it, her future could be a very cruel one." Numb with disbelief, David and Diana listened as the doctor described the devastating problems Danae would likely face if she survived. She would never walk, she would never talk, she would probably be blind, and she would certainly be prone to other catastrophic conditions from cerebral palsy to complete mental retardation, and on and on. "No, no," was all Diana could say. She and David, with their 5-year-old son, Dustin, had long dreamed of the day they would have a daughter to become a family of four. Now, within a matter of hours, that dream was slipping away.

Through the dark hours of morning as Danae held onto life by the thinnest thread, Diana slipped in and out of sleep, growing more and more determined that her tiny daughter would live to be a happy, healthy young girl. But David, fully awake and listening to additional dire details of their daughter's chances of ever leaving the hospital alive, much less healthy, knew he must confront his wife with the inevitable. David walked in and said, "We need to talk about making funeral arrangements." Diana felt so badly for him because he was trying to include her in everything, but she just wouldn't listen- she couldn't listen. Diana said, "No way! I don't care what the doctors say. Danae is not going to die! One day she will be just fine, and she will be coming home with us!"

As if willed to live by Diana's determination, Danae clung to life hour after hour, with the help of every medical machine and marvel her miniature body could endure. As those first days passed, a new agony set in for David and Diana. Because Danae's underdeveloped nervous system was essentially raw, the lightest kiss or caress only intensified her discomfort. They couldn't even cradle their tiny baby girl against their chests to offer the strength of their love. All they could do, as Danae struggled alone beneath the ultraviolet light in the tangle of tubes and wires, was pray that God would stay close to their precious little girl. As the weeks went by, Danae did gain an ounce of weight here and an ounce of strength there. At last, when Danae turned 2 months old, her parents were able to hold her in their arms for the first time. The doctors continued to gently but grimly warn that her chances of surviving, much less living any kind of normal life, were next to zero.

As if willed to live by Diana's determination,

Danae clung to life hour after hour,

with the help of every medical machine

and marvel her miniature body could endure.

Danae went home from the hospital, just as her mother predicted. At age five, Danae was a petite but feisty young girl with glittering gray eyes and an unquenchable zest for life. She has no mental or physical impairment. One hot, summer day near their home in Irving, Texas, Danae was attending her brother's baseball game. She was sitting on her mother's lap in the bleachers when she suddenly fell silent. Hugging her arms across her chest, little Danae asked, "Do you smell that?" Smelling the air, detecting an approaching thunderstorm, Diana replied, "Yes, it smells like rain." Danae closed her eyes and again asked, "Do you smell that?" Once again, her mother replied, "Yes, I think we're about to get wet. It smells like rain." Still caught in the moment, Danae shook her head, patted her thin shoulders with her small hands and loudly announced, "No, it smells like <u>Him</u>! It smells like God when you lay your head on His chest." Tears blurred Diana's eyes as Danae hopped down to play with the other children.

"No, it smells like <u>Him</u>!

It smells like God when you lay

your head on His chest."

Before the rain came, Danae's words confirmed what Diana and all the members of the Blessing family had known in their hearts all along. During those long days and nights of her first two months of life, when her nerves were too sensitive for them to touch her, God was holding Danae on His chest. It is His loving scent that she remembers so well.

Now years later, Danae is a thriving teen. She is healthy, intelligent, and quite musically inclined. This true story has been circulating world-wide for years via computer and has been published in several books. The Blessing family receives calls from around the world to confirm the validity of the story. Her father states, "She really has an unmatched walk with God." It is no wonder Danae walks so closely with God, considering the circumstances of her birth and the unshakeable faith of her mother!

CHAPTER FOUR

VALUES AND PRACTICE

—⟨ᴏ⟩

Treat others the way you would have them treat you.

Matthew 7:12

A nurse's value system affects nearly every professional or inter-active decision she makes, because it is a guideline for how to view and treat people in general whether dealing with patients, co-workers, superiors, or loved ones. The values within a clinical nurse affect how she treats her patients. A nurse in management has a responsibility to shape and fertilize those she supervises with life-giving words and supportive actions. The leader puts herself at the service of her staff. The reality is that the role of service becomes greater the higher we get in the realm of leadership.

The leader puts herself at the service of her staff.

The role of service becomes greater the higher

we get in the realm of leadership.

Sometimes a nurse's personal values correlate with those of the institution and sometimes they differ. One long-term care nurse shares, "The nursing facility where I work values giving good patient care, maintaining a home-like atmosphere, meeting all the physical and psycho-social needs of the residents, and maintaining compliance with all governmental regulations while simultaneously remaining fiscally solvent. My values align with all of these. When conflicts arise, they can almost always be traced back to the limitation of resources, especially manpower, imposed by the institution and the bureaucracy surrounding it."

Most employees are expected to accomplish more work than they are capable of completing, a fact which extends from front line employees all the way to upper management. When task and project-completion focused activity competes with people-friendly activity, conflict arises. These conflicts can even be morally and ethically challenging. Dignified, appropriate treatment of employees and patients should never be sacrificed at the altar of bureaucratic goal attainment.

Dignified and appropriate treatment of employees

and patients should never be sacrificed at the

altar of bureaucratic goal attainment.

THE VALUE OF HUMAN LIFE

The most extreme personal value faith-filled nurses develop in their lives and career is the value of human life. Every patient counts no matter what the age, status, or medical history. It takes a conscious, intentional decision to develop this value throughout one's career. This effort leads to an appreciation of every patient, even if he/she might have a colorful criminal background or an array of grotesque diseases. It also leads to a deep appreciation of many cultures and languages, as well as a respect for customs in other cultures and religions.

The first tenet of the official American Nurses' Association (ANA) Code of Ethics supports this concept of valuing human life. It reads, "The nurse, in all professional relationships, practices with

compassion and respect for the inherent dignity, worth and uniqueness of every individual, unrestricted by considerations of social or
economic status, personal attributes, or the nature of health problems." [1] This tenet can be viewed as applying to both patients and
co-workers since it clarifies "in all professional relationships." The
ANA incorporates more than the patient in this tenet. Although we
are all human and fall short of observing these values one hundred
percent of the time, we can still strive for better compliance and
continuous self-improvement. It is important to see our shortcom-
ings and those of others as opportunities for learning, and maintain
a tolerant, forgiving approach toward ourselves and toward others
when addressing them.

> The compassionate nurse blends the painful
>
> events in her own life into solidarity with
>
> others who suffer.

This effort to value human life creates a sensitivity and compassion toward individuals who are hurting, physically or mentally. In
a sense, the compassionate nurse blends the painful events from her
own life into solidarity with others who suffer. A nurse develops
beliefs about suffering that help in coping with continuous exposure
to patients' suffering as well as any sufferings that come along the
way in her own life.

THE VALUE OF A CO-WORKER

> Our greatest resource is always people.
>
> No form of technology or modernization
>
> can replace people.

Another extreme personal value faith-filled nurses develop is
that of appreciating co-workers, each one a priceless individual.

51

Our greatest resource is always people. No form of technology or modernization can replace people. Loyalty toward even the lowest-ranking individual should be given. It is important for leaders to intentionally develop the skill of sharing sincere compliments and observations with co-workers. When someone expresses a sincere observation or compliment with another, the recipient then chooses to receive it or reject it. Hence, the observations shared by other people contribute to their self-concept formation.

I can live for two months

on a good compliment.

Mark Twain [2]

As human beings, our self-concept becomes a collection of observations others made about us in the past. Sometimes we choose to take ownership of such observations, other times we may not. Thus, we can potentially have a significant impact on the development of character and values in others, simply by voicing our observations with them. When the nurse chooses to be life-giving and share positive things in the lives of her co-workers, good can result. One nurse explains, "I have found that these co-workers appreciate my appreciation of them, because they can see that I am looking at their internal value, not their external as the majority of society does."

Anxiety in a man's heart depresses it,

but a kindly word makes it glad.

Proverbs 15:30

In my many years of Nursing, I have seen many hardened hearts develop over time both in faculty members and nurse administrators. As the distance between these leaders and the patient increases, the Caring often seems to diminish or disappear entirely. Caring must be a decision for a nurse, whether she is a new graduate at the bedside, an experienced educator, or a director of nurses. We cannot allow our Caring to be affected by the surrounding circumstances of the moment. We have to strive to care in every moment of our practice, whether it involves a co-worker or a patient.

A cheerful glance brings joy to the heart.

Proverbs 15:30

THE VALUE OF NURSING THEORY

Many nursing students (and even some faculty members) feel that studying nursing theory is next to torture. I have found that examining the common elements within nursing theory reveals the complexity of what we do as nurses, but find that acting as nurses is much easier than dissecting the theory behind Nursing. Theoretical constructs, however, help us to organize and understand what we do and also help us gain new insights.[3] Studying nursing theory enhances and improves our daily practice, thus enhancing the nurse's overall contribution to human affairs.

Many find that acting as nurses is much

easier than dissecting the theory behind Nursing.

There is one particular, contemporary nurse theorist named Rosemarie Parse who writes about understanding the experiences in life which comprise the patient. I don't know if Parse realizes how Biblical her theory, the *Theory of Human Becoming*, really is.

To summarize it in my own words, a human person is an ever-changing sum of all his past experiences making each person a unique combination of his physical, social, psychological, and spiritual history. His dimensions are interwoven, and the present and the future is yet unwritten history for him. Therefore, life remains unpredictable. He is continuously "becoming" as life happens "to" him and "at" him. The challenge for the nurse is to try to empty herself of the things within that keep her from understanding the place where a particular, unique person or patient is at in this life journey.

Parse sees the nurse as really trying to put herself in the patient's shoes in every way. She makes herself present to that patient not by putting him in a box or category, but by really trying to accept and understand his current situation in light of where he is coming from, where he is at present, and where he wants to go with his health, his family, and his life. The exchange that happens between the nurse making herself truly present to her patient can itself be very therapeutic, simply because the patient perceives that he truly is being loved, understood and accepted without prejudgment.[4]

We would assume Parse experienced her theory in clinical practice before she began to write about it formally. Nurses today continue to experience the essence of her theory in living color every day in their practice. Any nurse can arrive at many of the same conclusions as Parse by simply pursuing personal growth in the traditional Judeo-Christian ways that many folks have done throughout history.

One perfect contemporary embodiment of Parse's ideals is Mother Teresa of Calcutta. She was a nurse in every sense of the word, although not formally educated in Nursing. She emptied herself of all pre-conceived notions of the stigmatized lepers of Calcutta, and devoted herself wholly to them. She sought only to help them to die with dignity, experiencing true love. Her efforts won her the Nobel Peace Prize which she used for the benefit of her patients. I have been inspired by the works of Mother Teresa since my childhood. I have tried to model my nursing practice after her.

She emptied herself of all pre-conceived notions

of the stigmatized lepers of Calcutta,

and devoted herself wholly to them.

She sought only to help them to die with dignity,

experiencing true love.

I believe that there are varying degrees of intensity in the act of being present to the patient. The area where this clearly happened for me most often was in Labor and Delivery, especially in cases where patients were deeply committed to having the least-invasive, most natural childbirth as possible. There were no shortcuts for them. I had to meet the woman at each and every stage of her labor process in unique and creative ways. I had to grow with her as her labor progressed, pulling from my bag of tools all the psychological, spiritual, verbal, non-verbal, tactile helps I could muster. I had to adapt my approach to the unique needs of any given patient. Sometimes a multi-para would act as if she wrote the book on labor and hardly needed me. Other times, I could have a primi-para who needed me every inch of the way. Still yet another with maybe a history of abuse, might need me in yet another completely different way. In other words, I had to be present to different patients in different ways. The end result for me, after giving entirely of myself to a delivery such as this, was usually a great deal of satisfaction (and a great deal of exhaustion). The patients usually were extremely grateful for the process as well.

I had to be present to different

patients in different ways.

THE VALUE OF THE POOR AND DISENFRANCHISED

I once had a "Mother Teresa moment" years ago in Juarez, Mexico. I went to Texas for a "working vacation." An outreach team from El Paso was planning to transport and distribute food to the poor in Mexico. I had the privilege of joining them.

TREASURE ACROSS THE BORDER

It was the middle of the night. We crossed through Mexican customs from El Paso into Juarez, harboring our precious cargo: food. There were butchered chickens and huge rounds of home made goat cheese on board with us.

The angels protected us as we prayed to avoid an inspection. If inclined, the inspectors could take the food and send us back. It was an uneventful passage. We thanked the Lord for His protection. When we arrived at a huge slum area called The Dump, the cold, pre-dawn mesa air penetrated our bodies. We prepared for the day. People were emerging from the darkness everywhere to line up in the food distribution line where out-reachers were bracing themselves in the cold wind for a long day of scooping. Yes, scooping- one portion of dried beans after another, all day long.

The food lines already were overwhelming, even before dawn. They were filled with a variegated, colorful mosaic of people: men, women, children, and elderly. The diversity of color was not intentional. You see, these folks were wearing all they had, in layers and combinations to protect their skin from the morning cold. There were no fashion statements or any sense of style in their vestments, only pure, practical function.

I was embarrassed to see a grown man wearing a full length set of pink, "footie" pajamas that I had only ever seen on toddlers at cozy bedtimes after a warm bath. I thought to myself, "How absolutely humiliating. Could this man possibly feel any dignity whatsoever?" I hoped inside myself that he knew how valuable he is to Our Lord. The line stretched hundreds of yards before him. He waited in his humility. The sun finally poked over the distant horizon with an array of pinks and oranges that only the angels could describe. The volunteers began to distribute scoops of dried beans to each of their guests in line. I was assigned to the women's clinic to help with patients there, and distribute the cheese to the pregnant and nursing mothers.

Hours of scooping had already passed as the bitter morning cold was replaced by the scorching heat. No one in the endless line shed their clothing, even in the parching heat, because they could not risk losing them. The man in the pink pajamas finally reached the beginning of the line by mid-afternoon. He approached the large sack, as a volunteer poured a full scoop of dried beans into a cloth the man held out. He disappeared into the crowd, taking his precious cargo along. Where he went from there, we will never know.

The volunteers left that tiresome day with a lot more than they had arrived with. They had the privilege of serving Our Lord in every person they had aided. Most Americans believe that treasure lies on our American side of the border. If only more people knew that the True Treasure lies on the other side- serving Him in the form of the poor.

Most Americans believe that treasure lies

on our American side of the border.

If only more people knew that the True Treasure

lies on the other side- serving Him in the

form of the poor.

THE VALUE OF HUMAN DEATH

Powerful things happen for a nurse when she chooses to reverently appreciate a patient as a valuable, sacred living being. Years ago, we received an admission to a nursing center where I was working. The man was a cancer patient, who also had sustained a self-inflicted gunshot wound which severely damaged a side of his head and neck. Coupled with the trauma were his cancerous lesions which also needed attention. It was a miracle that he survived. He was hanging onto life by a thread when he arrived from the hospital to the nursing home where he would die.

Powerful things happen for a nurse when

she chooses to reverently appreciate a patient

as a valuable, sacred living being.

GOD'S PLAN FOR A DIGNIFIED DEATH

When we received our new patient, he was weakened and debilitated, yet remained alert and oriented. He communicated by writing. His pain was under control by medication. The staff soon realized that there was a heavenly reason he was with us, and an intentional reason we were with him.

There was a heavenly reason he was

with us, and an intentional

reason we were with him.

I saw the nurse manager scramble to prepare her staff for the gruesomeness of this case. She worried that this might be too much for the staff psychologically. It took days of tender nursing care to have him finally properly cleansed and feeling human. I saw nurses, aides, social workers, and managers all go the extra mile for this man. They treated him like a king and gave him excellent, dignified care.

I wanted to reach out to this man myself in some special way. I assumed he might need to face God with the reality of his suicide attempt, in repentance. I wanted to share the Gospel with him without preaching "at" him. I wanted to give him a message, not from a one-dimensional, three by five tract. I wanted to be a three-dimensional, warm, loving, breathing, living witness to the Truth for him.

I searched my mind and heart for how to help him, in love. I mused about his Italian last name, thinking, thinking. Considering his cultural background, I thought to myself,

"I'll bet he had a very devout grandmother who would want him to have a rosary in these, his dying days."

I searched my mind and heart for

how to help him, in love.

I woke early the next morning. With rosary in hand, I visited a resident priest in the facility to bless it. I explained that there was a patient dying who needed it. He was more than happy to oblige. Now, I was ready to greet the suffering man. I knocked on the door. Awkwardly, I approached him in the bed and said, "Good morning Mr. DiVenezia. I, I, I have something for you that I thought your grandmother would want you to have at this time in your life. It is even blessed by a priest." He looked at me with a puzzled expression (even through the bandages) and wrote on his notepad, "Who sent you?" I wasn't ready for that question. I stuttered and scrambled for an answer and replied, "I was just really, really, inspired to do something for you." He solemnly looked down at his notepad and wrote, "Thank you." As he looked back up, I could see a tear begin to roll down his bandaged cheek. He wrapped the beads around his wrist and held the cross in his hand as if to cherish his gift. As I departed, I said, "I will be keeping you in my prayers. May God bless you."

The staff seemed to catch on that this man needed spiritual help. They called a priest to come for a pastoral visit and a peace came over him. They nursed his physical wounds, too. Nurses stepped up to the plate and frequently changed his dressings, which he needed, for the wounds were heavily draining and worsened by the cancerous tissue. Tears streamed from his eyes for the way the staff tenderly cared for him and touched him. He appreciated everything. We saw his demeanor change from the struggling and anxious to the serene and peaceful.

It is when we forget ourselves that we do

things that are most likely to be remembered.

Unknown Author

The Hospice nurses, having known this patient for months, shared that they had never seen him so well cared for. And to think we almost missed the opportunity and privilege to care for him. We were convinced that this man was miraculously spared an early death from the gunshot so we could have the privilege to care for him and so that he would have the time he needed to face himself and God prior to his death.

THE VALUE OF CHOICES IN DEATH

Healthcare workers sometimes

find themselves square in the middle of

a family's dysfunction at its very

climactic worst.

With all the tremendous medical advances in the healthcare arena of today, healthcare professionals find themselves involved in ethical cases more and more frequently. Just because all kinds of life-saving and life-sustaining means are available, does not mean that every measure should be used in every case. Discrepancies between people arise when those involved cannot agree on exactly where to draw the line of intervention. These discrepancies can arise between the patient, individual family members, the doctor, the nurse(s), clergy, etc. Additionally, the whole mix can be embellished with family dysfunction including anger, guilt, depression, substance abuse, and/or denial. Healthcare workers sometimes find themselves square in the middle of a family's dysfunction at its very climactic worst.

Today's older nurses originally practiced under the philosophy of saving life at all cost in their younger days. For me, as I grew older and started to accept my own mortality realistically, I began to change my views. I began to see the value in the acceptance of impending death. I began to see that death can be a comfortable, peaceful process when it is embraced instead of battled. Seeing that my own views took time to evolve, I do realize that maybe I shouldn't expect all society to be comfortable and realistic about mortality instantly.

Death can be a comfortable, peaceful process

when it is embraced instead of battled.

Due to growing limitations of reimbursement by managed care and the finite amount of fiscal resources available, healthcare providers need to be increasingly involved in educating patients and families regarding futile treatment. They have a moral and ethical responsibility to do so. Article II of the Human Rights Act from 1998 explains that our right to life does not include the right to a treatment that is not likely to be successful according to the judgment of a clinician. It also emphasizes and supports the right to dignity, even dignity at the end of life. Patients have the right to refuse or withdraw from therapies such as radiation, dialysis, hydration, nutrition, chemotherapy, and artificial ventilation.[5] Personally, I agree that patients should have these rights and nurses should do all they can to promote these rights and educate people about them. We often see patients unknowingly persist in treatments that are not likely to be successful which rob them of any quality of life, what little life they have left, as they succumb to their demise regardless.

The option for no treatment or intervention at all should be considered as a reasonable option in cases more often. Choices such as these can improve the quality of death. Is it taboo to discuss manipulation of factors that will affect or prolong a patient's death? Many providers are as uncomfortable with discussing quality of dying as some patients and families are to hear about them. Society cannot afford to preserve life at any cost economically, nor is it in the best interest to prolong life for many patients morally. Providers need education and awareness of these ethical roles they have with patients, and also need to grow comfortable with explaining to patients and families that certain requests may be unethical or inappropriate to carry out.[6] Providers more easily recognize the limits of medicine and need to share this expertise so patients and families better understand. Interventions that are not likely to benefit a particular patient must be more readily recognized as futile.

A CAREFUL DECISION IS MADE

I witnessed a situation where a patient made a choice about his life, ready to embrace his afterlife. He was a priest and was well loved by the community in a large, rural area. He made a decision to discontinue his hemodialysis and was dying of renal failure in the nursing home where I was working. It was a beautiful, peaceful death. I was privileged to be a part of the process, as there were many miraculous and celestial events associated with it. This event not only proved the value of a suffering and dying human life, but gave me a greater respect for life beyond the boundaries of this world as well.

THE FUTURE OF FUTILE TEATMENT

The issue of futile treatment is likely to mushroom over the next few decades because a precious, large group of our population, the Baby Boomers, is on the brink of senior citizenship. As this group ages and succumbs to such disorders as cancer, diabetes, heart disease, dementia, and strokes, there is likely to be a rise in the numbers of ethical situations involving futile treatment issues. An onslaught of diabetes and its complications may lead to an increased demand for dialysis treatment centers and the expense of these services.

The Baby Boomers did not know the dangers of smoking until they were adults. There may be health challenges related to smoking in many of their futures. The avalanche of health issues that will start affecting healthcare as the Boomers age will significantly exacerbate the need to address futile treatment in the future. These issues are never going to go away. As a result, the amount of time required for society to learn to accept and promote graceful and dignified death will be significant. Providers will forever remain challenged in the area of quality of life and quality of death. The more we learn about this topic and the more we sharpen our abilities to relate to people on these issues, the better we will be able to address this future wave of activity.

Providers will forever remain

challenged in the area of quality

of life and quality of death.

The greatest societal/cultural force in this ethical dilemma is ignorance (lack of knowledge) on the part of the public. People are greatly ignorant of end of life issues, quality of life issues and the realities of poor prognosis. We saw this in the Terry Schiavo case. Much of the media portrayed her as if she had been a person with no brain waves, dependent on a ventilator, one who would die the minute all plugs were pulled. It proved that the public does not understand the degrees of debilitation and medical need. In addition to the ignorance, end of life decisions with families are often riddled with denial, guilt, anger, and control issues. Sometimes expensive medical treatment is employed to treat families rather than patients. There is tremendous room for improvement in the area of advanced directives and educating others about them.

Sometimes expensive medical

treatment is being done to treat

families, not patients.

More nurses need to see that education of society regarding end of life care and quality of death is paramount because it will improve the dying process for so many patients and give them dignity in their death. Nurses' greatest contribution to society regarding any ethical and legal issues, including end of life, is education of the public.

FATHER AND SON

I once cared for a gentleman who had decided to discontinue his dialysis nearly two weeks earlier. He had depended on this life-saver for many years prior. He was beginning to show periods of confusion and some changes in his behavior as the toxins accumulated in his bloodstream. His son nervously approached me at the nurses' station with concerns over his father's changes in condition. I explained that he should expect to see his father go in and out of this confusion.

Knowing that every man's deepest wound can always be traced back to his father, I was compelled to mention to the son, "If you have any important thoughts to share with your Dad, you may want to do it soon because you might not be able to catch him in a lucid moment much longer." His face crumbled in disappointment and he struggled to keep his composure. He replied gently, "I have already done that." Trying to hide his emotions, he quickly turned and walked away. I was relieved to see his wife was down the hall watching us, and waiting for him, ready to console him. I wouldn't have wanted him to have to be alone at that particular moment when he was accepting his father's decline and eventual death.

Death does not sound a trumpet.

African Proverb [7]

Nurses must continue to educate patients and families to be prepared with advanced directives and also to be aware of patient preferences regarding healthcare. Nurses need to be delicately honest about their patients. Oncologists and other physicians need to learn to be more honest about prognosis as well. Patients are dying before our eyes, and families sometimes don't know they are dying. Last minute good-byes are missed because families are misled about a patient's condition, thinking improvement is on the horizon. Much of it is simply unintentional miscommunication.

Patients are dying before our eyes,

and families sometimes

don't know they are dying.

Healthcare providers have a moral responsibility to be aware of and involved in the ethical and legal issues of today. Just as Solomon requested from God to be able to judge and rule with great wisdom, so must we. Although technology and science have brought us light years away from Solomon's issues of the Old Testament era, the timeless desire to seek such wisdom still flourishes centuries later. I believe nurses can contribute to this process by teaching staff, students, and families to have awareness of moral absolutes and to have the courage to voice injustices when they are evident. Whether they know it or not, healthcare providers are leaving little legacies all over the world when they educate others. They also may not realize the magnitude their educational influence is having on others, or the way their influence expands exponentially.

Whether they know it or not, healthcare providers

are leaving little legacies all over the world

when they educate others.

THE VALUE OF DIVERSITY

Madeleine Leininger is another recent nurse theorist who wanted to see nurses become extremely tolerant and unprejudiced. She birthed and developed the transcultural nursing field and she created the *Theory of Culture Care Diversity and Universality.* Some say she is the "Margaret Mead of the health field." [8] Leininger proposes that there are universal nursing elements of care in all cultures. After World War II, she saw very futuristically that nurses in America needed to begin to understand and adapt themselves to the special needs of the spectrum of cultures entering our country through immigration. She also saw how ill-prepared healthcare was to adapt to the new, sudden cultural challenges. She developed her ideas into a formal, official area of study including education, research, and practice and she began paving the way for the diversity training of today. Awareness and understanding of cultural differences helps the nurse to be able give more appropriate care.

Leininger's theory supports that all cultures have some similarities. The elements of social structure and worldview must be understood by nurses to promote better patient outcomes. Nurses need to promote the preservation of diverse cultures while adapting them to our type of healthcare, even if it requires some reshaping to make it work. It works as long as Caring remains the central focus. [9]

Rosemary Parse is yet another recent nurse theorist who writes on diversity. Her theory, like Leninger's, promotes an unprejudiced, tolerant acceptance of the patient no matter what the experiential and existential history may be. The patient arrives at the place of needing healthcare, and the nurse makes a conscientious attempt to customize her care according to what she knows of the patient's life history of experiences and cultural background. In response, the nurse attempts to serve the patient in the most appropriate manner possible.[10] The underlying philosophy of both theories is the same overall: nonjudgmental acceptance of the patient.

The underlying philosophy of both

theories is the same overall:

nonjudgmental acceptance of the patient.

These theories of Leninger and Parse, although similar, differ in that each encompasses the acceptance of the patient in a different way. Parse's theory supports an acceptance of the individual patient as a unique person (of any culture) with a unique set of past experiences dictated by the randomness of the way life happened for the individual. It is as if the person was originally a blank hard-drive which life chose to fill with experiential "programs" to make up who and what he is today. On the other hand, Leininger turns her eyes to the backdrop of the patient's culture which includes an already established set of qualities and characteristics that existed within the culture before the patient was ever born. The nurse assigns these cultural attributes to the patient as she would for any other patient of that particular culture. Hence, both theories help nurses customize their care for the patient.[11]

I wonder if Parse and Leininger realized that they were taking cues from the Original Diversity Trainer of 2,000 years ago - Jesus Christ. Jesus demonstrated and promoted radical tolerance of diverse people all throughout his ministry. The Good Samaritan parable shows an undesirable stranger who stops to help a man suffering on the side of the road. Jesus found value in the gentile woman who drew water from a well for Him to drink. It was first a shock that He even bothered with a woman, much less a gentile woman, and she was subsequently converted. Jesus called upon Matthew, a crooked tax collector despised by his fellow Jews, to follow and serve Him. Quite oddly, Jesus had a surprising tolerance for even the Romans and the oppression the Roman Empire imposed on the Jews. He made it very clear that He was not here to be a political savior to remove the oppression of the Roman Empire but instead He came here to set people free from an even greater oppression, their own sin.

Cultural Diversity has always fascinated me, even as a child. I was fortunate enough to have all four sets of great-grandparents and both sets of grandparents alive when I was growing up. Each set came from a different European background, most were original immigrants. Some spoke no English, while others used English as a second language. Many of the customs, traditions, and dietary practices were transmitted to me. I was truly endowed with a great treasure of ethno-diversity, simply by virtue of my birth for which I am very grateful.

We all live under the same sky, but we

don't all have the same horizon.

Konrad Adenauer

This exposure to diversity continued as I attended school and began to be exposed to even more cultures. I recall using Leininger's Theory (without even knowing it) when I was working in Alaska in the Indian Health Service, serving the American Indian and Eskimo populations there.

OUR BIG, BROAD WORLD

I began to learn there were big differences between the Alaskan Indian and Eskimo cultures. There were also differences between the various types of Eskimo and Indian tribes. Their beliefs and practices are fascinating. They must be understood for a nurse to even be able to begin to care for these folks with any effectiveness.

There was once an old Tlingit couple I knew. The gentleman was in the ICU on a low dose Dopamine drip to maintain his blood pressure. I was trying to make therapeutic conversation with the patient and his wife. I was telling them that I was learning how to pick the wild berries that are so prevalent in Alaska and I was experimenting with making jam. This couple, full of sage advice, told me that when I go to the woods to pick berries, I should talk out loud to the bear. I should tell the bear that I was going to pick in a certain area and they could stay in a different area and neither of us would bother the other. The couple claimed that the bear is part human and can hear what we are saying even now. They also proudly stated that they never had any bad encounters with any bears in all their long lives while picking berries because of this fool-proof method they used. I knew I should graciously accept their advice and not try to contradict their ideas. I was practicing Leninger's suggestions without having learned them yet.

DIVERSITY IN CUSTOMIZING CARE

Understanding and applying nursing theory can help nurses to customize care for each patient. Nurses use facts and data gathered about patients to perform the greater process of interacting interpersonally with patients to promote wellness. The nurse helps her patient best by interacting well with him. An example might be the birth process. Even though I understand the stages of labor and the mechanics of delivery, my greatest aesthetic contribution to deliveries is the teaching, coaching, and encouraging I did for my labor patients. These activities put the women at ease and helped them to better employ the psychological powers of labor which promoted safer deliveries.

The nurse helps her patient best

by interacting well with him.

There are two nurse thinkers, Chinn and Kramer, who write that the patient is at the very least, the sum of his parts.[12] Knowing this, I have tried to view patients holistically in my practice. I believe it is more accurate to say that the whole patient is greater than the sum of his parts because of the strengthening and synergy that happens with all parts connected. This is especially true when including their spiritual component. For example, there is a big difference between the needs of one labor patient who has had several uneventful deliveries in the past with no losses and another labor patient who has had

69

multiple infertility problems or losses in the past. Seeing the entirety of each patient makes me alter my approach to each and how I plan to educate and encourage each during her labor process.

We know that society and culture dictate norms and guidelines that influence our behavior and shape us as individuals. Some environments promote health and wellness better than others. For nurses today, knowledge of diverse cultures and societies has been necessary for the delivery of effective care to patients.

AN APPROACH TO IMPROVE COMMUNICATION

In the 1980s, I was working for an inner-city hospital as a nurse on a medical/surgical unit. I frequently cared for Hispanic patients experiencing a language barrier who were not able to communicate their needs. Translators were hard to find. Many of the patients were HIV positive and kept in isolation a few days until tuberculosis was ruled out. The isolation, coupled with the language barrier, often left them unattended. This was before the days where regulations demanded mandatory translation capabilities in hospitals and the big push for diversity training.

Already able to read and write Spanish, I decided I would become more fluent in speaking so I could better care for these folks. I volunteered for an outreach in the Dominican Republic and learned the language by immersion. Thus, both the American and Hispanic cultures have influenced my practice by making it even richer with this diversity. I would encourage all nurses to embrace the richness of all the cultures and diversity their practice affords them. It is a privilege to have this exposure to such variegation in our practice.

I would encourage all nurses to embrace

the richness of all the cultures and diversity

their practice affords them.

HEALTH BEYOND THE PHYSICAL

Our concepts of health in the history of nursing have greatly impacted the way we practice nursing. Nursing has been, still is, and will always be about promoting health. Nurses not only address the physiological health of patients, but their psychological, emotional and spiritual health as well.

HIDDEN LOSSES, HIDDEN GRIEF

I once assessed a client who was being admitted to a 28-day drug rehabilitation program. Along with the lengthy physical assessment, I was concerned she might have a difficult withdrawal period. Emotionally and psychologically, the client had suffered a history of abuses and lost custody of her children. She also had unresolved grief issues.

As I took her gynecological history, she revealed she had experienced an elective abortion at age thirteen which her parents forced her to have. I noticed that suddenly, it was more difficult for her to volunteer information to me. Now crying, she continued to explain that she wanted to have and love her baby. She was forced into the procedure. She explained, "I didn't really understand what was happening to me. I was so young. I called the clinic the next day desperately asking for my baby. I asked them where my baby was and they told me I wouldn't want to know. She went on to explain that she became very promiscuous thereafter and began to try to ease her pain with drugs, alcohol, and men. She had other children who were in state custody and other abortions thereafter as well. She hoped the drug rehab program would help her to rise above her tragic circumstances.

Intuitively, I recognized that maybe she was suffering Post-Abortion Syndrome (PAS) along with all her many other diagnosis. PAS involves the psychological impact of an abortion on a woman after the experience. Some experience a type of post-traumatic stress disorder related to a past abortion and its impact. Even men can experience this when they have been powerless to defend their unborn child's life.[13] Knowing that these rehab patients uncover, reveal, and address many devastating and hurtful events of their lives in their group sessions and workshops, I suggested that she might want to make sure she addresses (rather than represses) the pain and unresolved grief surrounding her abortion. I emphasized that this program is a safe place for her to share about this. She told me she was surprised and stated, "No one has ever even mentioned that my abortion could be a part of my problem." I just encouraged her and mentioned I would be praying for her. I could only hope those 28 days would be a healing time for her. Our society doesn't generally expect nor permit grief after an abortion.[14]

CHAPTER FIVE

FAITH AND SCIENCE

Every worthwhile gift,

every genuine benefit comes from above.

James 1:17

CAN FAITH AND SCIENCE BE BEDFELLOWS?

Florence Nightingale had the right idea when she saw science complementing faith instead of opposing it. She pioneered nursing theory, having no prior theoretical foundation in place to build upon. She clearly defines health, the patient, the nurse, the observations, the science of Nursing and the art of Nursing. The patient is located at the center of her model. The health of the patient is more than merely the absence of disease but also holistically includes environmental, physical, and psychological aspects. Nightingale saw the nurse as any woman who tended the sick, invalids, infants, or children, even well children.[1] To Nightingale, observations included any data or details noted by the nurse's senses and they were carefully recorded, measured, and studied statistically. Thus, Nursing was viewed as a science. Nightingale's approach to

Nursing as an art included her more spiritual and aesthetic view of the profession.

Nightingale's ideas were relevant in her day,

and remain relevant in ours.

As theoretical constructs should,

they have survived the test of time.

Nightingale's ideas are valid because the concepts are applicable to both the Victorian Age and to the 21st Century. Take, for example, Nightingale's encouragement of a holistic approach to health. In recent years Americans have considered the same, turning more and more to alternative medicines and nontraditional methods of promoting wellness. Health visits include a thorough inquiry about alternative herbs, supplements, and practices. Nightingale's ideas were relevant in her day, and remain relevant in ours. As theoretical constructs should, they have survived the test of time. It is wise for nurses to continue to review her constructs and gain her timeless insights.

The conflict between science and faith is unfounded. Just as Nightingale viewed science as a complement to her view of God [2] professionals today can maintain this same view. Science is congruent to faith and spirituality, not in opposition to them. Every new mystery in nature uncovered by science reveals a new wonder of God. The Creator expected us to appreciate Him more deeply as science generated tools for us to understand His works more intricately over time. He knew that time would hand us the magnifying glass, the microscope, and later the advanced telescopes and electron microscope. He knew satellites and today's technology would be part of the mix. He knew we would have entire libraries of information at our fingertips. Perhaps God intended for us to be able to uncover the mysteries of His creation gradually over time so we could grow to know Him better in an incremental way as mankind took up each new tool and God was further revealed with each.

NURSING AND TECHNOLOGY

One element of science, highly advanced technology, is a more recent trend in society which is affecting nursing practice immensely, especially the areas of diagnostics, documentation, communication, and education. Access to the Internet makes for more self-educated patients which also means healthcare workers have to accommodate the new challenges that ensue from more informed (and sometimes misinformed) patients.

The technology of the past thirty years has affected the relationship between the individual and society in both professional and personal ways. In the home and in the workplace, technology has brought positive enhancements and also negative deterrents to the life of the individual. These effects then ripple out from the individuals to impact our society as a whole.

Some of the technologies that the average American has adopted over the past two decades include a personal computer, a cell phone, digital planners, computers in the workplace, and digital photography. In the workplace, such devices have enhanced capacities for the dissemination of large amounts of information to larger groups of people at much faster rates. Once employees are trained on how a new piece of equipment is implemented, organization and efficiency are expected to improve. These improvements and monetary savings are measured and categorized. Systems are streamlined and simplified. Both new terminology and new etiquette have emerged to accommodate this new communication medium. Abilities to do and share research also have expanded immensely.

With all this new technology, however, face-to-face communication dwindles and there is not as much opportunity to practice the personal touch and person-to-person courtesy. The individual misses the chance to communicate with facial expressions, body language, and genuine concern for others when most messages become digital. As a result, the workplace is depersonalized. Accurate first impressions and the ability to make eye contact are nearly gone, intuition in the presence of another is less often practiced, and leaders have fewer opportunities to praise and encourage subordinates in person. Hence, workplace morale and company loyalty can suffer, as individuals see themselves more like independent contractors in someone else's environment. It is not as common to view oneself as an integral part of a greater whole. Sometimes it helps to make little excursions to ask co-workers questions or to clarify things instead of writing the thoughts in an e-mail or making a phone call. It can be an effort to communicate and network better. When I do this, it gives me a chance to see these individuals and read if they are content or struggling. Can I see how they are feeling? Do I see pain, worry or stress? Do they seem rested or comfortable? Does their color look healthy? I offer to help problem solve if someone appears distressed or stressed.

What is somewhat lost in the workplace

is the personal touch and opportunities

to practice person-to-person courtesy.

At the personal level, the individual today has new options for communicating with loved ones and friends, too. Cell phones and text messages are very common. For example, the parent can track and monitor his teen with a cell phone much more easily than in the past. Plans and meeting places between family members and friends can be made more conveniently. Messages and pictures can be transported around the world inexpensively. Travel plans can be streamlined and facilitated online for family connectedness.

Formal education has been made more affordable and more accessible since the advent of distance learning. Some parents, discouraged by the deterioration of their local school systems, find that the personal home computer makes home schooling a viable and effective alternative for their children. Working adults also have more convenient and accessible continuing education possibilities available to them than ever before in history.

For the creative individual, the personal computer has opened up a new art medium. Computer art, course design, and web design are all ways for the expert or the novice to express their artistic side in a new and expanding medium. As word processing has been refined over time, the potential for expressive writing and publishing have become more available to the average individual.

The computer and the Internet have revolutionized the world of merchandizing and consumer purchasing. The glass windows for window shoppers have been replaced by millions of digital windows subjected to the beckoning call of someone's fingertips. Products are more easily showcased to larger viewing populations and consumers are able to view and purchase more conveniently.

Several problems have evolved with the greater usage of technology in some peoples' personal lives. Cyber-crime has forced the individual to adopt more ways of protecting his identity and financial information. Increased use of the Internet by average Americans promotes easier access to child and adult pornography by the young and adults alike. There are web-sites available for pedophiles to share and learn techniques. Pornography addiction continues to take its massive toll on marriages, relationships, and the safety of our young. These impact the physical health, mental health, and well-being of individuals.

Society as a whole is affected greatly by the new technologies adopted by individuals. Whether or not these technologies have produced true forward progress is a different debate. The negative ways people chose to use modern technology are proof that the universal vice of greed will always remain, as Christ predicted. He knew there would always be the poor because He knew there would always be the greed. Greed can foil even the most carefully engineered processes, systems, and strategies. But this will not deter those determined to continue to seek improvements for the greater good of all. Let us honor those who persist in inventing, creating, and improving new technologies all in the name of positive progress!

The universal vice of greed will always

remain, as Christ predicted. He knew there

would always be the poor because He knew

there would always be the greed.

Another negative impact of technology impacting education is the increasing inability to see the instructor as a live role model in a traditional classroom setting. There is no substitution for the live, face-to-face example. We have all learned under instructors that we would want to emulate and we have experienced those that we would not. Some of their behaviors we have adopted as our own. A course does not only exist for covering the volumes of content. There is much more for students to learn like the professionalism, manners, respect, intuition, integrity and other virtues in a scholarly educator. The live classroom exposes students to a role model they can emulate. Young students today may be experiencing a deprivation of these bonus features of education.

The students need to witness the

professionalism, manners, respect, intuition,

integrity and other virtues in a scholarly educator.

Good nursing educators make sure technology is used as a tool and does not become an end in itself. They do this by viewing their students as unique individuals comprised of increasing varied and valued characteristics, life experiences, and formal education. Learning upon learning is happening for each student in unique ways. If instructors keep this personal appreciation of each student in the forefront, it should keep the technology from superseding the learning.

THE INFORMATION AGE

We are in the midst of a technological explosion where our life itself is being revolutionized by the technology of today's Information Age. Technology impacts communication, data management, and access of information in all fields, especially in healthcare. Information access has a dramatic affect on education by making healthcare education more accessible, even from great distances.

Such technology improves healthcare in many ways, but creates new challenges in other ways. For example, many healthcare workers do not even understand the difference between electronic health records and electronic charting. An electronic chart is a component of the larger electronic health record. Clashes in simple definitions such as these assault effective communication. We have people starting out on different pages, confused from the outset of the process. How can the outcome be successful if the beginning starts with confusion? We know that nearly every conflict or problem can be traced back to a root cause of some type of communication mishap, with or without technology.

We know that nearly every conflict or

problem can be traced back to a root

cause of some type of communication mishap.

Nurses in clinical practice need to take a closer look at their capabilities in using technology. If there are heavy limitations there, education is knocking. Nurses cannot be afraid to learn or change. The best way to let go of old, stubborn attitudes is through education. As a person breaks the barrier of ignorance, that is "lacking knowledge," the benefits and conveniences of technology soon become evident. It just takes that initial leap of faith to step out of one's comfort zone to learn something new.

TECHNOLOGY IN NURSING EDUCATION

Like many other things in life, technology

is safe when kept within

appropriate boundaries.

Moderation is so often the key.

There are still great differences of opinion among seasoned educators in learning institutions about the value and adequacy of online learning.[3] Some of these professors perceive overall technological change as an element to be resisted. But technological change is an element to be accepted as both necessary and inevitable, especially in the world of education. Like many other things in life, technology is safe when kept within appropriate boundaries. Moderation is so often the key.

It is proven that nursing students in and from high technology educational settings do better in their healthcare positions of today and tomorrow than the students from less technological nursing programs. [4] Professors and instructors need to be highly competent and supportive of technology in nursing education if they want to generate competent nurses. For example, a nursing program with various clinical sites presents the opportunity for the students to examine multiple electronic charting systems [5] thus giving them exposure to a variety of systems which can equip them to be able to adapt more fluently to their future nursing positions. They will be more flexible and informed than their counterparts because of the prior exposure.

Nursing educators need to embrace every aspect of technology and get as familiar with it as humanly possible, whether they agree with it or not. They are doing a disservice to the students if they don't. Technology will march on with the students either dancing with the beat or crawling to catch up, depending on how they are taught.

Technology has also positively impacted nursing education through the growing availability of instantaneous, massive amounts of information. For example, in the early 1980s, library books were still catalogued in a card index and shelved. A student was limited only to the books, articles and periodicals held by that particular library. Some information was stored on awkward microfilms, and anyone doing serious research had to spend days and even weeks just to find the desired information. Today, the average household can access thousands of entire libraries from their home instantaneously.

There are also many ways in which technology has negatively impacted nursing education. One way is the depersonalization in the classroom. For example, in an online course, faceless students and professors (if any) interact without the benefits of observing facial expressions and body language or hearing voice tones. Learning this way has its positives and negatives. The positive of convenience and availability of courses contrasts the negative of invisible classmates and professors. Students must weigh their options and choose carefully, and instructors must be aware and sensitive, maximizing the best circumstances for each teaching moment.

Instruct a wise man,

and he becomes still wiser;

Teach a just man and

he advances in learning.

Proverbs 9:9

CHAPTER SIX

NOTABLE TRENDS IN HEALTHCARE TODAY

— formula—

It is important for all of us to try to make

people feel important for who they are,

not for what they can or can't do.

POSITIVE TRENDS

Any nurse practicing for ten to fifteen years or greater has had the opportunity to observe some positive trends in healthcare take root over time. Confidentiality practices have improved. Patients have become more consumer-driven with improved access to information and greater understanding of their health management. In recent years, seasoned nurses also have seen a trend toward greater patient self-care.

CONFIDENTIALITY

The Health Insurance Portability and Accountability Act of 1996 (HIPAA) is a public law that came from Congress in order to ensure that individuals with pre-existing medical conditions cannot be refused health insurance when changing jobs. It was primarily designed to address the driver of access. Congress did not want individuals with pre-existing conditions to be denied medical insurance when changing jobs because Congress knew that insurance provides the ticket to access medical care. Health insurance opens the door into the healthcare system.[1]

HIPAA has also been very effective in the way it influenced another driver, quality. We witnessed a huge wave of new confidentiality practices take root in our physicians' offices, dental offices, hospitals, rehabilitation centers, nursing homes, and every other type of healthcare facility. Staff Development nurses began to implement HIPAA in-services and continue to do so. Awareness spread. State and joint commission inspectors probed to insure that sensitive patient information became much more secure. There has been a very positive effect on patient confidentiality, hence enhancing overall quality.

HIPAA has greatly influenced nursing practice. Nurses are much more careful and discrete with patient information, both verbal and written. Bedside paperwork, such as an intake and output sheet, is managed differently. They are enclosed in folders or binders. A shredder or shred box is located at each nurses' station as a common practice now. Nurses are more attentive to where they discuss patient information, making sure no one can overhear the discussion.

SELF CARE TRENDS

Dorothea Orem is one particular nurse theorist who writes extensively about patient self-care. She wrote the *Self-Care Deficit Theory*, which is very useful in nursing practice. Patients needing nursing care require it in differing degrees such as wholly compensatory (greatest need), partly compensatory (some need), or supportive education (information need).[2] Therefore, the nurse is giving total care, partial care, or teaching at any given moment.

Patients originally were treated as passive recipients of healthcare. They depended on the healthcare professionals to decide what care was needed and provide it. As our society became more consumer-driven, patients have taken a more active role in their care decisions. Providers began to educate patients more. Patients began to educate themselves more. Studies began to show improved morale of patients who had been afforded more influence on their own care. Healthcare learned that patients want self-determined healthcare in varying degrees depending on how sick they are. Generally, the sicker a patient is (as in advancing from partly compensatory to wholly compensatory), the more willing he is to leave the decisions up to someone else, [3] which is where the nurse's role as patient advocate expands.

The sicker a patient gets the more

willing he is to leave the

decisions up to someone else. [3]

One important facilitator prevails in the growth of this self-determination by patients with their healthcare process: American consumer-mindedness. In recent decades, Americans have become better "shoppers" in all areas of commerce, including goods and services. This mentality easily crossed over to the healthcare arena and was embraced by patient consumers. Patient satisfaction surveys are taken very seriously and addressed. The result today, hopefully, is a much more user-friendly service. Even when the patient himself is not able to advocate for himself, many times the families or responsible parties step in as consumers and advocates.

The long-term care arena has evolved and improved tremendously since the 1970s. Today we care for our residents in a much more dignified manner and weave more patient self-determination in the process. Patients are involved in their care decisions as much as they are mentally able. Food and clothing preferences are honored. Patient rights are openly posted and known by all. Nurses orient themselves to a dementia patient's reality instead of trying to orient him to her reality. Residents and families participate in care planning and family meetings. Resident Council meetings are held regularly, and their concerns are addressed. Choices are given and preferences are honored. There is a complete culture change happening in long-term care.

As patients became more self-determined, the main challenge for nurses was taking on a greater role of both educating and listening to patients. Nurses needed to learn how to discuss options more extensively and respect patients' informed decisions. In addition, nurses had to learn to draw the family into the equation for decision-making. Nurses today are better prepared to answer questions or find the answers they cannot supply immediately.

Orem's Theory is useful and appropriate when applied to self-determination of care. It is not a stagnant concept tucked away on a book shelf, but rather is alive and dynamic. It weaves itself through nearly every aspect of healthcare and has survived recent changes within the system as healthcare became more consumer-driven.

Orem also promotes an interesting way of looking at people. She identifies all humans as falling within two categories: those needing nursing and those producing nursing.[3] We could conclude from this outlook that we are doing one of two activities at any given moment: needing care or giving care. Those needing care require it in different degrees such as greatest need, some need, or information need only. Hence, the nurse is giving total care, partial care, or teaching. Here we are back in education. Even when we are not at work formally educating a patient, we are educating the "well" people we encounter inside and outside the healthcare arena. For example, I encountered a woman in church one morning leaving the sanctuary in tears. I asked her if I could do anything for her. She said, "I don't want my son to see me like this. It will scare him. I've been sick lately. God has touched me today for the first time since I've been sick." I told her gently that it might be good for her son to see her leaning on God in this way so he will know to do the same when he is troubled. She really appreciated the observation when she realized it was an opportunity for her son to learn. The nurse helps in the community even when she is not on duty.

I told her gently that it might be good

for her son to see her leaning on God.

Dorothea Orem's Self-Care Deficit Theory has informed my nursing practice in the past and continues to do so today. She says that nursing has three features including the professional-technical, interpersonal, and societal.[4] I have seen myself evolve in all three areas, even in that same order. For example, remembering my focus in college and as a new graduate, the professional-technical aspect dominated my concerns initially. I see this today with clinical students or new graduates. I was drowning in a sea of information and afraid of all I didn't know. At that stage, I was so concerned with doing everything by the book or I might harm a patient. As I grew more comfortable in my skills, my eyes turned more readily to Orem's interpersonal feature of nursing. I could do the technical skills almost on auto-pilot and relate to the patient and family at the same time. My multi-tasking abilities began to grow.

Where do the seasoned nurses go?

Once I had grown competent in the professional-technical and interpersonal, I gained a history of experience and wisdom easily identified in the "seasoned" nurse. I must say, these nurses are harder and harder to find these days. Where do the seasoned nurses go? They don't go, but they grow into Orem's <u>societal</u> feature of nursing. They enroll themselves in college or graduate school so they can make a better contribution to nursing and society as a whole by becoming better educators, mentors, and leaders. Seasoned nurses try to compound their efforts exponentially by influencing the groups they lead or the students they teach, realizing that life is shortening and they must pass the torch to the next generation.

We know that different developmental age groups have varying degrees of need in their condition of self-care deficit. Orem categorizes patients by how dependent they are. The pre-born (antepartum), infants, and some of the elderly are totally in need and therefore wholly compensatory. Children and some adults are partly in need and therefore partly compensatory. Those who are self-sustaining have minimal self-care deficit and need mostly education and information. One deficiency in Orem's theory may be the fact that the unborn, infants, some elderly, and some chronically ill children and adults remain in the wholly compensatory mode for extended periods of time and are not capable of *any* type of self care. These are the least suited groups for application of her theory. Orem's theory might apply best to those in partial need.

OUR MOST VULNERABLE

The patients who fall in Orem's wholly compensatory group are the most vulnerable and weakest members of our society. It is very easy to neglect them without it ever being noticed. Since my earliest years in nursing as a nursing assistant in the 1970s, I have noticed a great improvement in the area of dignity, especially in the way we care for the elderly. Back in those days, restraints were everywhere, pureed food was fed to patients via 60cc syringes, people were fed with the staff standing and rushing. Alzheimer patients roamed with the general population of residents, etc.

Today we care for our residents and patients in a much more dignified manner. Alzheimer and dementia patients are safe behind secure doors together. Their special needs are met by specially trained staff. We feed the dependent properly, slowly, seated, and making conversation. We avoid words like "bib" and "diaper" using "clothing protector" and "brief" instead. We give them choices and try to deliver their preferences. We listen to their voices in Resident Council meetings and are open to their suggestions. In other words, we try to treat them with dignity even though they have a self-care deficit. It is important for all of us to try to make people feel important for who they are not, for what they can or can't do.

DIGNITY IN DEMENTIA CARE

The evolving changes in dementia care practice are dramatic. In the early 1970s and 1980s, dementia patients were considered "senile" and poorly understood. They were mixed in with other alert residents in the nursing home as roommates and neighbors. As the body of knowledge about Alzheimer's and other dementias grew and the pharmacology improved, nursing practice for the dementia patients improved. The evidence was gathered through both quantitative and qualitative research and it reflected both scientific and intuitive knowledge. For example, empirical, quantitative data regarding the use of restraints and data about elopements, falls, injuries, and deaths was considered. Qualitative research was also done that included information about observed and studied behaviors of dementia patients.

When both forms of research were gradually compiled, a better method of nursing management of dementia patients evolved. Today we can asses a patient and see how far advanced their disease is. We provide enclosed units where the wanderers are able to wander safely. Nutrition and hydration are closely monitored. The same staff members are used for care as much as possible to reduce agitation and anxiety. The individual concerns about each patient are known so as to reduce the incidence of agitation by meeting their needs early or ahead of time. Validation within patients' delusions and misconceptions is used to allay agitation. Properly titrated medications are making a world of difference. There are fewer falls and injuries since restraints were decreased. Dementia patients are better understood as staff members are specially trained and receive continuous educational updates. Improvements are constantly added. Families are more in the loop and receive more helpful information. Thank goodness for those who invested their time and efforts to promote improvements in dementia care through research and dissemination of the information across the world.

OUR BLESSED BOOMERS

America is graced with a wonderful, large population of adult Americans who are about to start their transition into their senior years. By the year 2010, more than 39 percent of Americans will be 65 and older. By the year 2020, the rising percentage will be greater than 53 percent and by 2030, more than 69 percent. In short, our senior population will double within the next fifteen years. Massive social change is starting and longevity is creating a revolution in our society. The trend of growth in the population of elders coupled with the trend of rising costs of healthcare give us plenty of incentive for developing health promotion and disease prevention programs.[5]

Our future seniors, the Baby Boomers, are the most educated generation in history and this education and knowledge impact the choices in lifestyle they make.[6] This population will be more likely to initiate solutions to their health challenges as they arise. Many of today's seniors are the parents of Boomers. The Boomers are a potential asset for today's seniors. An educational thrust toward them could be a worthwhile investment of time and energy for both today and tomorrow.

The Boomers in general are known to have sufficient fiscal resources. The demand for their optimal quality of life has already begun. We see this in the advertisements for products to promote sexual health and function as well as many types of anti-aging strategies. The old, familiar self-determination and individualism that dominated many of their lifestyles in the 1960s are resurfacing through the music and attitudes of today's advertisements aimed at them.

How can we, in healthcare, ever prepare adequately for the onslaught of healthcare needs this sector of our population will generate as they get further along in their senior citizenship? The Alzheimer Association predicts in its 2008 Facts and Figures Report that one out of every eight members of the Boomer population will have dementia.[7] Nurses have a moral responsibility to rise to all the health challenges the Boomer population presents us.[8]

One out of every eight members

of the Boomer population

will have dementia.[7]

A NEGATIVE TREND

One universal health issue that severely impacts America and the world at large is our poor, steady diet of detrimental programs on television and other screen media. Children and adults alike are viewing mind and value-shaping ideologies that are not always the healthiest for them. When Pope Benedict XVI was speaking to the youth in New York during his visit to America, he shared about a particular, sinister, somewhat unnoticeable area of darkness. This is the detrimental area of darkness which affects our minds:

> *"The manipulation of truth distorts our perception of reality, and tarnishes our imagination and aspirations. I have already mentioned the many liberties which you are fortunate enough to enjoy. The fundamental importance of freedom must be rigorously safeguarded... Yet freedom is a delicate value. It can be misunderstood or misused so as to lead not to the happiness we all expect it to yield but to a dark arena of manipulation in which our understanding of self and the world becomes confused or even distorted by those who have an ulterior agenda.*
>
> *Have you noticed how often the call to freedom is made without ever referring to the truth of the human person? ... What purpose has a freedom which, in disregarding the truth, pursues what is false or wrong? ...Dear friends, truth is not an imposition. Nor is it simply a set of rules. It is the discovery of the One who never fails us; the One in whom we can always trust. In seeking truth, we come to live by belief because ultimately truth is a person: Jesus Christ. That is why authentic freedom is not an opting out. It is an opting in; nothing less than letting go of self and allowing oneself to be drawn into Christ's very being for others."*

> *Pope Benedict XVI*[9]

One common example of how minds have been altered in our society is the way that Hollywood's idea of feminine beauty and sexuality is pounded into the heads of females and males alike, leading many women and girls down that dark alley of eating disorders and self-esteem problems. The way this spreads across our globe is through the television itself. The television is both the vector and mode of transmission.

Children and adults alike are viewing

mind and value-shaping ideologies

that aren't always the healthiest for them.

Our neighbors in the developed world and those in the third world have much of our American programming available with translations or subtitles. I have seen this first hand in Brazil, the Dominican Republic, and Mexico. I did a search of the data bases and found that there have been eating disorder studies done all over the world from Spain and the Mediterranean to Japan and Pakistan to Iran to Argentina to Germany to Russia, etc. People in other countries misunderstand that Americans behave and run their lives like the examples they see on television. The impact on women and girls (and even boys and men) throughout the world is similar. Women are struggling across the globe to achieve the American idea of beauty. I remember reading an article once that explained that cosmetics are even available to women in the Amazon jungle for purchase and delivery. How important is lipstick in the steamy jungle?

Women are struggling all over the world

to achieve the American idea of beauty.

One young teen shares her thoughts on the struggles with beauty and love:

Beauty & Love

Webster's definition of beauty is: the quality attributed to whatever pleases or satisfies the senses or mind. [10] *Although this definition is true, I believe a lot of us, as a youth, misinterpret the definition of beauty very often. In the world today, the secular meaning of beauty in a person is incredibly superficial. We've been taught that guys and girls are supposed to have perfect skin, perfect hair, perfect facial features and a perfect body, even if it takes putting yourself in harm's way to get it. Although self-appearance is important because of how strangers view us, it has nothing what-so-ever to do with beauty at all. Originally, beauty came from the meek and the loving, the selfless and the virtuous, the inside. Some still see beauty this way, but more and more of us are buying into the lies and deception from the enemy in his persistent goal to destroy us.*

So why do we contribute these confusing ideas about beauty to a surely already troubled mind? Being a faithful, Christian young man or woman in this world is simply hard enough...why make it harder by worrying about beauty? Of course we know that there is a deeper meaning to beauty than what the world recommends daily, but what is it really? To me, it really is a deeper meaning than a pretty face. It is all one Being, one Word and that Word is God.

Your adornment is rather the hidden character

of the heart, expressed in the unfading

beauty of a calm and gentle disposition.

This is precious in God's eyes.

1 Peter 3:3-5

Allow me to explain when I say that beauty is God, in a word. God is love so let's start off with love. If we were to try and find the superficial meaning of love today, it would be finding "the one." We know that if we focus our life on finding someone, chances are we're trying too hard and it will end badly because we're seeking something that we probably don't have with God. This is true especially if we are willing to compromise our morals just to be with someone. While falling in love is an amazing blessing, a lot of us get so lost in the pressure of finding someone that we forget the first form of love on this earth that ever existed which was the love between God and man.

In Genesis, it says that God created man in His image and likeness. This is only one of His innumerable acts of kindness, mercy and love. Even though we are a flawed and undeserving race, He still continues to show mercy and love to this very day. That alone is a greater love than any human being could ever show for another. This is why we, as individuals, should focus on our personal relationship with God more than anything else.

He hath made everything beautiful in his time.

Ecclesiastes 3:11 KJV

Boyfriends and girlfriends come and go in our lives, but we will always have God there until the death, and even after death. It is safe to say that investing in a relationship with God is much more beneficial and concrete than a maybe or a could be. I'm not saying that God does not want good, fruitful relationships and love to come about in our lives, but it's all in His timing. If we are struggling in our love life, or we feel like the world is crashing down on us, and we are praying, wanting, and asking but not receiving anything, or have been given what we've asked for but it wasn't what we thought it would be, maybe we should do less talking and more listening. Sometimes there are still things we have yet to learn, and sometimes God even calls us to be single. Whatever it may be, and whatever He calls us to do, we always have to keep in mind that He always has our best interest at heart. He loves us and wants to see us happy and flourish and grow, and He will find a way. Even if current circumstances blind us to what God wants, we just have to trust like we never have before and obey and submit and give ourselves up to His will.

So many suffering people in this world would lessen the load on their backs if they just tried to trust God little by little. There where times in my life where I was just not happy because I chose not to listen to what God was trying to tell me. I wanted to believe that something I thought would work out eventually would, and that it was what God wanted even though it was clear that it was the complete opposite. It drew me inward, and I slowly started to eat away at myself, desperate for anything that would substitute for what I lacked. In the end, I was thankful that I realized that I needed to trust God and that He cared about me so much as to do everything in His power to lead me back on to the right path, back into His forgiving arms. I was so busy looking for artificial forms of love when I was ignoring the Greatest of them all. Sadly, I also even know adults that are still continuing to relapse in this lack of trust over and over again, and every time they turn away, they sink deeper and they wonder why but it all leads back to the same thing: listening. It's good to pray and run to God when we are troubled and are having problems but sometimes He doesn't always answer our prayers for a reason. It's not because He doesn't love us or He doesn't care. It's really the complete opposite.

I was so busy looking for artificial

forms of love when I was ignoring

the Greatest of them all.

Love is such a strong word but I think sometimes we forget what it truly means because we use it so liberally in our daily lives. I also believe that true strength is often misinterpreted as well. We have a God who is so magnificently dedicated to loving us, yet we fail to see this. Have you ever loved someone selflessly and tremendously and then watched them crush your very heart before you? To be Christian would be to forgive them, no matter the pain or the cost but do we truly? This is also something I believe we have all struggled with in our past at a certain point in our lives. Someone hurt you and you claimed to have forgiven them, but in your heart you were still utterly disgusted but did not know how or why or with whom. Some of us even get so lost that we secretly seek revenge in return but we know it is not healthy so in a sense, we get a sort of release from annoying them or talking about them behind their backs. In this case or any other where we are faced with the temptation to bring someone down, even ourselves...we have to remember that the more time we spend talking about people and bringing them down, the less time we spend loving them. It would most definitely be unfair if we didn't forgive others and love them with all that we have when we have a God that does that exactly and perfectly.

Great you are, Lord God!

There is none like you, and there

is no God but you, just as we have

heard it told.

2 Samuel 7:22

We must strive to love and forgive, and that doesn't mean that we have to love what a person does, we just have to love the person. Numerous times in our lives, we strike a blow to someone's heart, someone who has loved us unconditionally from the very second we were brought into existence without having anyone there to tell Him to do so. Is God not hurt when we choose to go against His will? Yet He still continues to love us, through our every sin and wrong decision that we make. So too must we be with others and of course it will be hard, it's life. We weren't exactly guaranteed an easy life, but the point here that I'm striving for through this example is love. True love that never falters, and is never changing and will always be concrete, <u>always</u>. We *can only strive to imitate and share this completely perfect love and completely perfect example as a flawed race. We must pray that we never, for a second in our short lives, forget this love. This strong foundation of devotion, Caring and selflessness never goes unnoticed and if we are loved and we know that we have love in our life. It isn't because we were given it; it was because we gave it.*

Our love is nothing if we do not give it. So instead of turning to other things, why don't we just follow God's example and love? This unchanging and unfathomable love is also the pure definition of strength. Through every little sin we commit, every blow to His heart, He takes every single one without complaint. His love still remains and this is true love, this is true strength.

So shall the king greatly desire thy beauty:

for he is thy Lord;

and worship thou him.

Psalm 45:11 KJV

We can just get lost in thought sometimes because of how everything about God is so uniform and organized and beautiful, all working together for the greater good. It's indescribable how He is so many wonderful things combined. He is justice. He is forgiveness. He is strength. He is humbleness. He is hope. He is infinite. He is so many things but above all, He is love and in this completely divine love, I see true beauty in its greatest form. None of us could even begin to comprehend Him fully. He is intangible, yet we are constantly surrounded by Him. This is the most beautiful mystery I've ever known.

He is intangible, yet we are

constantly surrounded by Him.

At the end of every road of every false desire, He's always there, waiting patiently. He is waiting every time we stumble. He's there to pick us up. He is true beauty. He was the first form of beauty and will always be. If we just strive to be more like Him - gentle, humble and meek, our efforts will be rewarded. The inner feeling of being justified will suffice because we know in our hearts that it is right and although it's more difficult than anything in this day and age to go against what everyone else follows, in the end it really saves us so much pain. If we just strive for holiness daily and follow Him in His grace, we can only hope that maybe some of His beauty will rub off on us too.:)

Maria Rey, Age 16

One thing I ask of the Lord: this I seek:

To dwell in the house of the Lord

all the days of my life,

That I may gaze upon the loveliness of the Lord

and contemplate his temple.

Psalm 27:4

MORE ON THE SCREEN

Other examples of the detrimental effects of television and screen viewing could also include the sedentary nature of the act itself. The greatest factor contributing to our American health is lifestyle. Lifestyle dominates all other factors at 50 percent. Next, environment and genetics, tied at 20 percent each. Medical factors only comprise 10 percent of the pie! [11] How many Americans succumb to an overly sedentary lifestyle related to television or screen viewing? Aside from the bodily inertia, the content of these screens impacts the way many Americans think and behave. How great is the impact of viewing violence, sexual content, crime, and mistreatment of others?

Behavioral science could help us study and measure more information about this topic. The public could be educated in the findings, and cautioned appropriately. Policies and guidelines already are in place that rate programs according to levels of violence, language, sexual content, and age appropriateness. The choices are in the hands of the individual. Just as a person chooses between the hamburger and the garden salad in his nutritional diet, so he must choose what he will digest in his mind in front of the screen menus. Mother always said, "Garbage in, garbage out!"

Boundaries enhance sexuality.

The screen promotes every form of sexual activity everywhere and with anyone. The screen is robbing the public of the ability to realize that boundaries enhance sexuality. They are being coerced into accepting a counterfeit to the authentic sexuality their Creator originally developed for them. This intrusion is affecting peoples' sexuality both physically and psychologically. We have seen how America and countries across the world have struggled to curtail the spread of AIDS and STDs over the past several decades. What a huge endeavor it has been to try to alter the behavior of the public so as to protect them from these disease threats. We are in the midst of a collective teachable moment in our history. [12] Promoting more educational and tasteful program development and encouraging healthier screen viewing choices might be a great start to improving not only American health but world health, in both the physical and psychological sense.

We are in the midst of a collective

teachable moment in our history.[12]

HEALTHCARE REFORM: CURATIVE TO PREVENTATIVE

There is an attempt to shift the healthcare model from the acute model to the preventative model evolving today. Each health profession has an integral role. One profession cannot do it alone. Rather, it must be a combined effort of nurses, physicians, pharmacists, dieticians, technicians, social workers, case managers, counselors, leaders, administrators, and educators. The proper attitude is one that sees each of these disciplines as a necessary partner in this process of healthcare reform. With various healthcare professionals looking through the spectacles of their own profession and fending for their own territories and roles, one might ask, "Who is left to advocate for the healthcare consumers? How is quality of care ensured?" One advocate for consumers is the government, upholding regulations and standards that safeguard care. This is why regulations and standards are important. When issues are being addressed by a variety of healthcare professionals collaboratively, their context is expanded and there is greater understanding among disciplines.

Who is left to advocate for the

healthcare consumers?

Healthcare reform requires much patience on the part of its members. Although we live in a world of much instantaneous activity and instant gratification, there are no quick fixes for the problems in healthcare. Complaining does not help either. Even when solutions to any problem seem very logical and simple, it still takes a great deal of time to process change. When a nurse understands policy making, she will have more patience and respect for the whole process. Solutions can only come about through the proper channels of policy making or amending.

When a nurse understands policy making,

she will have more patience and respect

for the whole process.

As with any type of change in any organization, healthcare reform can only move forward successfully if it is done in incremental stages. It has to be strategic. Part of the strategy includes focusing on the healthier populations for disease prevention, such as children. Stakeholders are more likely to accept and adopt smaller incremental changes rather than one massive, instant overhaul. In order to maintain health and prevent disease, the populations that are still healthy must be reached with good health maintenance information. The time and effort invested now could save on cost and resources tremendously in the future. The old cliché, "an ounce of prevention is worth a pound of cure" is a timeless principle and will always ring true.

CHAPTER SEVEN

CARING IN NURSING EDUCATION

_____꧁

The ability to make change happens in the classroom.

Hubert Humphrey

There is plenty of literature and there are many theoretical constructs available about nurses and Caring. What about faculty members and their Caring toward students? How much is required? What are the benefits? Just as faculty practiced Caring as novice nurses so, too, must that caring model be carried over into the classroom. An education works well when the learners commit themselves to learn well and the instructor commits herself to educate well. Commitment of self to students, in Caring, is imperative for educational success. Once a student knows how much the educator cares, then she will care about how much the instructor knows. A mentality of abundance will ensure that there will always be room to care more, whether it is at the bedside with a patient or in the classroom with a group of students.

A mentality of abundance will ensure

that there will always be room to care more.

The American Association of Colleges of Nursing created a document called the *AACN Position Statement on Defining Scholarship for the Discipline of Nursing*. This document states that the scholarship of teaching promotes the transfer of the science and art of Nursing from the expert to the novice, while bridges are built between both parties.[1] How better to build a bridge of trust between parties than through Caring?

How better to build a bridge of trust between

parties than through Caring?

Just as we try to be compassionate, empathetic, and caring with our patients as nurses, Caring can flow from faculty to students as well. Each student has a story. Each has a reason for entering Nursing. Each has wounds and healings. The instructor can look at the whole person, not just the student shell. She tries to hear all the things the student is not saying in words. Caring helps the learning to be more student-centered. Caring and student-centeredness are both other-focused. The instructor tries to put herself at the vantage point of the learner. Caring encourages our patients and our students to grow in their own spiritual journey. A teacher or instructor needs to be comfortable in her own spiritual journey before she can promote that of her patients or students.

Each student has a story.

CARING IN ACTION

Several fall semesters ago, I had to apply Caring to an extremely intense situation with a group of clinical students. They were nursing students in their first nursing clinical of a fundamentals course. We were all well-bonded and comfortable with each other by the end of the semester. I had been transparent and open with them throughout. They knew all sides of me.

The semester was coming to a close and the holidays were approaching when one of the students was killed in a car accident.

Immediately, I was thrust into a search for what was appropriate for me to do regarding the rest of the class continuing the remaining clinicals, the skills labs, the mourning, and the services. What was my role in helping the students? Where is the teachers' manual with the instructions for a scenario like this? I knew the students would be looking to me to help process the tragedy. I decided to write and share a eulogy at the viewing. I had been inspired. I hoped the students and the congregation would find solace in the words. It was much appreciated and the students felt it brought them comfort and a means to closure. It was a situation where I had to step up and put into action what I had taught them all semester.

ONE BRIEF EULOGY

On behalf of all the faculty and students of the college, I would like to express our deepest condolences to Janet's immediate family, and all her relatives and friends.

Twenty-five years ago, Janet was born. She brought much joy to her family and others as she grew. She was a delight and a pleasure to all who were fortunate enough to know her. I was blessed to meet Janet in her first nursing course at the college last spring and I was her clinical instructor this semester as well. She had a tremendous determination to complete the nursing program to become a nurse. Her faith meant everything to her in her life and in her calling.

Just a few weeks ago, while we were in the hospital together, I noticed Janet seemed upset and was trying very hard to hide her feelings. We sat down privately, and this is when I really learned how special she is. She explained to me that she is a Christian. She talks to God and she prays. She felt that God was helping her through her studies and all parts of her life. She wished she knew the secret to having others learn to do the same. She said that there was one particular person in her life that she was worried about not having a walk in faith. Maybe that person is you.

Her faith meant everything to her

in her life and in her calling.

We both pondered a while for a possible solution to her dilemma, and together we came up with the idea that the best way to introduce someone to God and start walking in faith was through prayer and by our example. Maybe we just rediscovered the concept that Francis of Assisi spoke of centuries ago. He said, "I preach all day long. Sometimes I use words." Janet, like Francis, felt that our actions spoke best for our faith. It's no wonder she wanted to be a nurse. She had given herself completely to God and to serving Him. She had given herself so completely, that even in her passing, she was able to help improve the lives of over a dozen patients receiving organ transplants.

Janet felt that our actions

spoke best for our faith.

It's no wonder she wanted to be a nurse.

Two thousand years ago, another beautiful Baby was born. This Baby was a boy. We celebrate his birthday every year without fail, because this little Baby became our hope for life both here on earth and beyond. It is very consoling for us to know without a shadow of a doubt that Janet put her hope in the beautiful Christ Child and what he later accomplished on the cross. The best way for all of us to honor Janet, is to fulfill her wish. Her hope was in her faith. Let us follow her example. Let us turn our eyes to Jesus, to look full in his wonderful face. Let us welcome Him the way she would want us to today, and this Christmas, so we can behold Him as she does.

ALL NURSES ARE TEACHERS, ALL NURSES ARE STUDENTS

Not every nurse holds a faculty position at a college or university, but every nurse is an educator. Nurses frequently function as preceptors, mentors, and patient educators. When we teach, we help patients and novices build new knowledge on top of former learning and leave them fertile for the future learning yet to come.[2] The educator has to know what the students already know, and where they have already been, so both teacher and students can go forward from there. The whole process is very learner-centered.[3]

Not every nurse holds a faculty position

at a college or university,

but every nurse is an educator.

We must remember students learn well from each other. Students need to be told less and allowed to discover more together. Content is much more the means to knowledge than an end to it. Content is for using, not just covering. Learner-centered teachers lecture less and are around the classroom more than in front of it.[4]

A nursing educator strives to gain a much deeper appreciation for the uniqueness of the individuals she instructs or cares for. Every person is a unique composite of features and characteristics different from any other person ever in existence. Discovery of learning styles and intelligence types adds to the hundreds of characteristics that help us to appreciate individuals as unique combinations of gifts and experiences.

Every person is a unique composite of features

and characteristics different from any

other person ever in existence.

ATTRIBUTES OF AN EXCELLENT EDUCATOR

There are several desirable core qualities found in excellent teachers. These include things like knowledge of the subject matter, being a good communicator, a stimulating style, an ability to relate the material to the student's world and actual experiences in real life, interest in the material,[5] enthusiasm for the material, an overall positive attitude, and a willingness to go the extra steps to promote learning.[6]

The excellent educator has respect for the students.[7] She demonstrates sincere respect for all the students and for people in general. She conveys a helpful, caring attitude. She is committed to the students and uses integrity and honesty in all her dealings.[8] When a nurse becomes an educator, she becomes "a nurse for the learners." The flow of Caring is shifted from educator to learner instead of nurse to patient. These ideas are congruent to the Caring Theory as proposed by Jean Watson. [9]

The excellent educator has

respect for the students.

Another attribute of an excellent nursing educator is her ability and desire to self-teach. Every nurse educator must be an informed educator. She is not afraid to tackle any new content and incorporate it into a course so she will have command of the subject matter within the classroom. She keeps herself challenged intellectually.

An excellent nurse educator must be genuine. She should not be afraid to express who she truly is. If one is trying to portray a façade, the students will quickly discover it and the teacher's credibility in the eyes of the students will be forever blemished. Animation helps immensely. A lively, expressive face and demeanor captures a student's interest more readily. These tie in with another important trait: passion for the information conveyed. An educator has to believe in the information they are selling to the buyers, the students. Another trait of extreme importance is care for the person within the student. Caring must be nurtured in the classroom between teacher and student.

Caring in an educational setting leads us to a timeless principle we call commitment. Commitment is important in nearly every aspect of our lives, including education. An infant survives because of the commitment of his parents to raise him. A marriage endures because two people are committed to maintaining and nurturing it. A person lasts in a job because there is a commitment and a contractual agreement to work. An education works well when the student commits herself to learn well and the instructor commits herself to educate well. An instructor should not be afraid to commit herself to her students, in Caring. There is always room to care more.

COMMITMENT

The classroom becomes a nurturing place

of self-discovery with the power

flattened throughout.

Commitment to education is not just a one-way process from educator to student. It is reciprocal. Teachers learn from students. For a student, education is a means of empowerment. She commits to the process voluntarily and the degree of learning is congruent to her degree of commitment to learn. As an educator, education is a means for continued, deeper learning through the sharing of knowledge and experience between educator and learners. The instructor does well to be a committed, genuine salesperson and display her passion for the information being sold. The instructor must promote student-centered learning and have the teaching styles complement the learning styles in any particular learning environment.[10] Student-centered education takes the educator role from the star on front stage to the assisting usher in the audience, guiding the participants in their common enchantment with the show. The educator is more around the classroom than in front of it.[11] The classroom becomes a nurturing place of self-discovery with the power flattened throughout.

An effective instructor is committed to being an approachable instructor. Students need to feel comfortable approaching the instructor with any concerns. Barriers to learning are identified and plans for overcoming them implemented. All student diversities are embraced and accommodated. The creative educator finds ways to employ a student's diversity as an advantage for the learner and her classmates. The different levels of nursing education are also included in learner diversity yet all of these nurse learners are on the same path of Caring. They only differ in where they choose to rest, stay, renew, or restart.

The creative educator finds ways to

employ a student's diversity as an

advantage for the learner and her classmates.

The wise instructor commits to being a life-long learner and a better critical thinker. She promotes the development of both aspects in her students as well. Students are told less from a faculty-dominated classroom and assisted to discover more of their own conclusions and connections. An instructor is addressing the whole student when promoting her critical thinking.[12] The educator sets a quiet but powerful example for the learners when they see her commitment to lifelong learning as a means for personal and professional growth.

Teach them to carry out everything

I have commanded you.

Matthew 28:20

SPONTANEOUS TEACHABLE MOMENTS

These "moments" often disguise

themselves as interruptions.

As an act of service when I go about my daily activities, I keep my antennae up for recognizing spontaneous, teachable moments that continually arise. These "moments" often disguise themselves as interruptions. (I do this at home with my children, too.) This occurs at every level. I might have information for an administrator, a nurse, a manager, a housekeeper, a security guard, an activities aid or a kitchen or maintenance worker. The staff developer should be concerned with everyone's continuous learning. Better educated employees ultimately yield better, caring service to the residents.

AN UNLIKELY STUDENT

I once conducted a Certified Nursing Assistant (CNA) Training Course where an Administrator in Training was required to attend the didactic portion. Instead of viewing this as a bother or a burden, I quickly realized that there was an opportunity to possibly impact hundreds of lives in her future administrative actions by how and what she would be taught in the course. I actually had a future administrator as a captive audience for an eighty-hour spontaneous teachable moment!

How many administrators or upper level managers in healthcare do you know that could use a lesson in Caring, dignity and compassion? If they are treating their staff with dignity, the staff in turn will treat the residents or patients that way. As usual, I kept Caring at the forefront of most topics as much as possible. Any point is valid in a nursing assistant class if the benefit and best interest of the residents are the goal.

The dynamics in the classroom were very interesting. Annette was a lively student participant. She asked ques-

tions, took the tests, studied, and learned skills in the lab, etc. I wanted the students to show respect for her as a leader in case Annette ever actually ended up as their adminis-trator! So, while we were learning, I called upon Annette to share her administrative expertise in the areas with which she was familiar. This showed the students that Annette is an administrative professional while also showing them that I respected her, too. It all worked out very well.

Annette came away from that course with a deep appre-ciation for all that nursing does. She rightly learned that the nursing assistants are some of the hardest working, under-valued employees in the building. She knows that <u>they</u> are where the rubber hits the road. They make or break a facility. This scenario set well with my conscience. It was an act of service where those benefiting were Annette, the other students, Annette's future subordinates and residents, and myself. It taught me to stay alert for other teachable moments on the horizon.

CHAPTER EIGHT

MORE HATS THAN SHOES

—⟨ℑ

Blessings crown the head of the righteous.

Proverbs 10:6

Most women think they can never own too many shoes. Have you ever bothered to count how many hats you wear as a nurse instead? Nurses have so many hats they wear in the different roles they perform that their hat collection can get larger than their shoe collection!

CLINICIAN

One role we see many nurses perform is that of the expert clinician. Nurses as clinicians need to make a strong effort to stay current on best practices, pharmacology, and technology. The nursing process must be used where appropriate as a guide for clinical skill and documentation. Excellent clinical nurses look toward evidence-based practice for improving their own clinical practice.

LEADER

The nurse's role as leader is infinitely important. The last chapter of the book is dedicated to examining leadership.

FOLLOWER

Nurses in the leadership role grow in their abilities and confidence. The excellent nurse leader is discerning enough to know when and how to be an effective follower. She functions independently, thinks critically and gets actively involved.

The excellent nurse leader is discerning

enough to know when and how

to be an effective follower.

The effective leader must have a background as a strong follower so she can understand the followership of those that she leads. Good followers are able to work independently. They do not need to be micromanaged. Just give them the job and they'll get it done. Followership and leadership are inseparably intertwined. They are directly dependent on each other.[1] To be a leader without followers is simply impossible.

There are many strategies for becoming an exemplary follower. Such followers are involved in continued education, ownership at the practice site, mentoring and the practice of assertiveness skills. Followers are willing to embrace and accept the role as leader. They are inquisitive and probing. They ask more questions to better understand the roles and functions of their subordinates and colleagues. They appreciate them as assets to the organization.

TEACHER

Nurses often find themselves in an array of teaching roles. They teach patients, families, co-workers, orientees, and new graduates. Nurses as faculty members teach every facet of Nursing.

> Great satisfaction is earned when an
>
> educator learns how to first recognize
>
> and then seize the teachable moment.

From Erikson's well-known Stages of Human Development, we know that individuals in the stage of middle adulthood have a need to create a living legacy in their children or the next generation.[2] If one spends her entire adult life exposed to and employed in the healthcare arena, it's easy to see why a need to contribute to the next generation of healthcare workers ensues in the middle of a nursing career. Great satisfaction is earned when educators learn first how to recognize and then seize the teachable moment. She takes advantage of the serendipity. Even greater satisfaction is received when a difficult topic is finally understood by a group of students after a painstaking presentation. A good educator presents information in a variety of ways so it can be understood by every type of learner, and also knows how to motivate students to get excited about what they are learning. It helps when the instructor is able to demonstrate the practical application of the information as it applies to the future practice of the students.

SCHOLAR

Good nurses strive to be good scholars. They are dedicated, life-long learners. Each is a continual work in progress. The nurse scholar strives to keep herself current in all content and technology which evolve over time in healthcare. It is very easy to fall behind in one's clinical skills and knowledge base. Older individuals of every profession are seeing that their former training is rapidly growing obsolete in the light of new technology, information and knowledge. Nursing is no exception. Nurses and educators alike are constantly striving to incorporate new technology into their practice. Once the technology is incorporated, it is often then better appreciated by the user.

CRITICAL THINKER

A nurse is thinking critically when she is processing and intellectualizing information and facts to guide her actions and behavior. Critical thinking involves a collection of many types of thinking: scientific, mathematical, historical, anthropological, economic, moral, ethical, philosophical, [3] and theological. The excellent nurse strives continuously to be a better critical thinker. Her thinking is growing increasingly self-directed, self-disciplined, self-monitored, and self-corrective. She puts her thoughts through the rigorous test of her high standards and she gains careful command of them. She knows how to keep egocentrism, sociocentrism, and ethnocentrism out of the equation. She is sensitive that her own biases may be trying to interfere with understanding other's views.[4] In other words, she develops the habit of controlling her thought life.

Nurses of faith know that the Apostle Paul recommends that believers handle their thought life cautiously:

Do not conform yourselves to this age,

but be transformed by the renewal of your mind,

so that you may judge what is God's will,

what is good, pleasing and perfect.

Romans 12:2

To the population at Philippi (and to us) Paul also writes:

...your thoughts must be wholly directed

to all that is true, all that deserves respect,

all that is honest, pure, admirable, decent,

virtuous or worthy of praise.

Philippians 4:8-9

The critical thinking nurse also tries to be a critical listener, speaker, reader, and writer. She is cautious about the message she communicates. She strives to make her communication clear, accurate, precise, logical, complete, significant, and fair. She is able to enter the perspective of her audience or listeners and see their perceptions from their vantage point. [5] This is the reason a sharp nurse embraces diversity. When she understands a person's ethnic and cultural root structure, it makes her better able to imagine their world and perceive the view through their eyes. The nurse doesn't understand others if she doesn't uncover, discover, explore, appreciate, and network with them.

Some of today's children and adults will be tomorrow's nurses. If society wants them to be able to think critically, we must acknowledge that American screen viewing impacts how people think. It is hard for anyone to refute the dangers of the screen media and entertainment as they insult America's collective abilities for critical thinking and intelligence. This includes both adults and children. If we are not careful, the pied piper within the screen can lull his passive observers (adults and children alike) to ignorance. How dangerous for America when her children cannot learn how to think critically! How can people act well if they cannot think well?

If we are not careful, the pied piper

within the screen can lull his passive

observers to ignorance.

RESEARCHER

Nurses can use their role as researchers to create positive change in healthcare organizations. Nursing research and all its evidence can bring about changes in practice when the right people are informed of the right facts. Regulations are imposed based on convincing research findings that support practice changes. The valid proving of ideas and the use of terminologies like "evidence, scientific, empirical, scientific knowledge, studies, and literature" are all part of research. Quantitative terms associated with numbers like "incidence, mortality, and morbidity" support ideas.

Intuitive knowledge and the qualitative aspects of supporting ideas are found within research as well. It is difficult to substantiate practice and policy changes with only intuitive knowledge or opinions. Changes and interventions take place so as to promote positive policy and practice changes that ultimately lead to better results for the greater good and greater numbers of patients (i.e. better outcomes overall). Many times, saving both time and money is also a desirable result in addition to the improved health outcome for patients. The recommendations yield desirable and positive results. These changes in practice need to be shared to become consistent throughout healthcare.

Favorable findings in one location are shared with others so that policy and practice changes help an optimal number of patients across the nation. That is why research needs to be duplicable and requires a standard method of dissemination. If we did not have guidelines, standards, and parameters for how to do and share research, we would have a confusing mix of chaotic information spinning around aimlessly in literature and cyber-space with no effective method for sharing new information to improve practice.

CHANGE MAKER

The nurse cannot passively accept what

the future is handing her. She must

carefully craft her own future. [6]

Nurses often find themselves leading change. The nurse as a change maker leads by example. She keeps herself constantly aware that she is a role model for her colleagues. She is compliant with facility policies and organizational progress. She battles the tendency toward inertia that plagues individuals throughout the healthcare arena. People are great resisters of change. Even managers and administrators are infected with this inertia. Many individuals find it difficult to see that there is always room for improvement.[7] The nurse cannot passively accept what the future is handing her. She must carefully craft her own future [6] and the future of her organization.

In any facility, everyone knows where the suggestion box is or how to suggest a change, but very often these resources either are underutilized or suggestions are misplaced or ignored. Change is the hardest thing to create. Motivation is a difficult thing to share. Every nurse has ample opportunity to practice the art of inspiring others to change and foster improvement in the healthcare arena of today and tomorrow. The war against this inertia must go on, winning one battle at a time, or the allies will all succumb to the disease.

CULTURE CHANGE AGENT

Nurses are in a great position to enhance culture change within healthcare organizations. Nurses influence many critical areas of practice directly and positively such as

o   patient outcomes and fewer errors, thus improved quality assurance
o   patient satisfaction, thus greater numbers of patients returning for services

o   communication and team work, thus improved efficiency and continuity of care
o   decreased costs because of improved efficiency and streamlining
o   recruitment and attractiveness of facilities, thus decline of staff shortages
o   employee retention, thus combating shortages offensively
o   decreased employee overhead cost due to improved recruitment and retention
o   contribution to the community at large, thus a healthier population in general

The above areas need much attention in our current healthcare system. All wise administrators would do well to look at the prospect of culture change in their organizations. The benefits are far-reaching.

ADVOCATE

Nurses have a moral obligation to advocate for individuals or populations who are subjected to any abuses or negligence. These include our patients, the elderly, the poor, some minorities, the children, and the unborn. Most nurses have no problem advocating for victims such as these. How many nurses notice that they have a moral obligation to advocate for each other? Nurses are notoriously passively aggressive and downright hostile toward one another. If nurses would make their Caring for each other a priority, Nursing and healthcare itself would be revolutionized.

CHAPTER NINE

NURTURING THE SELF GOD GAVE YOU

The truth is: most nurses take better

care of their patients and their children

than they do of themselves or each other.

In an ideal world, the nurse arrives at work well rested, has all her affairs intact at home so as not to interfere with her work, never needs to go out for a smoke break, has an ideal body weight and she maintains a healthy, consistent diet. The nurse in the ideal world always has the opportunity to actually take a lunch break. She successfully climbs the career ladder, does not need to take prescriptions to help with mood, sleep, or stress and endures a whole shift without any physical pain. In this imaginary utopia, nurses watch out for each other and run to each others' assistance. They encourage each other routinely. They are also immune to being scoffed at, ignored or demeaned by any other healthcare worker, especially their bosses and physicians. Sadly, I know nurses that would be tickled to have just two or three of these conditions satisfied. The truth is: most nurses take better care of their patients and their children than they do of themselves or each other.

ARE YOU MORALLY DISTRESSED?

Aside from all the challenging conditions of work, nurses also face moral distress there. This distress can start early in a career or arrive later. Most nursing students and new graduate nurses experience moral distress upon entering the field of Nursing. They have made a huge intellectual, emotional, and financial commitment to the field, and begin to question their vocational decision once they start to see the realities and constraints of Nursing in the clinical setting. Some begin to realize it before graduating, others after. For many, it happens in the early years of the career because nurses realize the limitations imposed on all the good, altruistic work they had planned for their patients. These nurses realize they are limited throughout the system by fiscal issues, staffing shortages, insurance challenges, mountains of paperwork, heavy assignments, and the list goes on. They begin to feel that their work is compromised by the effort to finish on time or nearly on time. They wish they could take better, more thorough care of each patient, but they settle for doing the best they can. They are torn between the textbook ideal and the bedside activity (or lack thereof) which they actually see happening. Some perceptive nursing students see the writing on the wall before they ever even graduate.

As a manager, preceptor, or educator a nurse may find herself trying to help a new nurse to recognize and cope with moral distress stemming from these shocking realities. When I find myself in this situation, I emphasize to the novice that they have choices to make. I explain that they will not always be able to perform textbook Nursing and I further explain that they need to find their own level of compromise that they can accept. Usually, they seem relieved to learn that complete perfection is not the actual norm or expectation and that every similar situation is not always handled the same way.

This phenomenon of disillusionment is very similar to other climactic events in our lives. For example, when we marry, we have a pre-conceived idea of what life will be like with this new spouse. After the honeymoon phase, disillusionment sets in and we get the chance to really exercise the promise of commitment that we originally made. The same can be said of bringing home a new baby. The pre-conceived idea of parenting is rapidly replaced by a realistic one, often accompanied by disillusion. The challenge of the infant becomes one of a toddler, a child, and continues through adulthood.

Nurses are constantly faced with choices

for right or wrong in their practice.

The rightness or wrongness of a nurse's actions depends on the nature of the acts as well as the consequences resulting from them. Nurses constantly face choices for right or wrong in their practice. The intent is for desirable, improved patient outcomes, yet the nature of the acts is just as important as the desired result. In Nursing, we are concerned about results as well as the manner in which they are achieved.[1]

STAFFING CONCERNS ARE CRUSHING NURSES

Staffing issues are a common problem in nursing practice. As healthcare evolved over the past decades, overall staffing ratios dwindled to sometimes seemingly unsafe levels. Middle management is often caught between loyalties toward good patient care and the administrative and fiscal demands of the organization. These middle managers wearily advocate for their subordinates and their patients. As for upper-level management, it is not uncommon to see a director of nurses endure less than two years in her position. Over time, you see her face fall, her shoulders slump, fewer smiles, and ultimately a desperate resignation.

Middle management is caught in a dilemma mixture of loyalty toward good patient care, loyalty toward efficient and effective staffing of units, and the desire to satisfy the administration by being fiscally conscious. Many clinical nurses struggle with disillusionment within their profession. By and large, nurses do not recruit their daughters, sons, or acquaintances to their profession. Many nurses succumb to the same diseases they have battled for their patients.

These conditions result from years of spiritual and bodily neglect and abuses: depression, fibromyalgia, chronic fatigue syndrome, the damages of smoking, obesity, diabesity, and all the diseases of unrelenting stress. Their motivation is lost, and they wonder when the disillusionment set in. Many are too easily reduced to objectifying their patients and their vocational calling to a mere paycheck.

FRUSTRATED WITH CONDITIONS?

Having known many nurses from a wide array of locations and specialties, I sat down one day to write a list of all the nurses I knew personally at that point in time. I listed their names and I counted attributes that I knew about each. Of the 112 nurses on my list, 48 worked for more than 1 employer, 47 were actively seeking a change from their current position to another somewhere else, 18 were furthering their nursing education formally, 13 worked for a nursing agency, and 6 were successful nurse entrepreneurs. Although this information could not qualify as legitimate statistical data, it does comprise a group of random nurses.

I concluded from an overview of these 112 nurses that a sizeable percentage of them (nearly half) were unsatisfied in their current work because of the fact that they were seeking change. Nearly half worked for more than one employer, which leads me to think they were seeking better control over where, when, and how often they work. Possibly, these nurses were simply trying to make better wages. I was pleased to see that at least 18 were formally furthering their education. Again, this hints of an element of control, as they took charge of their own career advancement. The six nurse entrepreneurs have completely taken control of their own employment situation. Each worked very hard, but each appeared to enjoy the autonomy. My hat is off to them.

The actions of these 112 nurses ring out one great message to me: "I want more control over my employment situation." Could their motivation come from a frustration with the status quo? Might they be seeking better wages? The fact that so many significant changes within the career (as in education and job changes) eludes that many were not content with what they were doing at that point in time.

HOW FRUSTRATED NURSES TRY TO COPE

Nurses in this disillusionment dilemma have several options. They can go job hopping for greener pastures, but lose seniority and longevity at their current place of employment, or they can change positions within the current organization. So many specialties are available in Nursing that nurses never run out of new areas to explore, which can distract them from their frustrations, and still keep them within the organization where they have familiarity and longevity.

Frustrated nurses could also take the approach of confronting the problem, quantifying it with supportive data, and by approaching administration with the findings. Valid points could be substantiated. The challenge would require much strength and fortitude, when most nurses are already maximized in their daily energy output and have little left for such a battle. There is also the possibility of effects on the home life as even more energies are spent fighting battles.

The Caring is the burning furnace

inside, ever fueling and driving

the momentum.

Clearly, the best option for creating the most good for the most people would be for nurses to gather their strength and confront <u>any</u> problem by approaching the right people with the appropriate information. An example might be data about the facility staffing patterns arranged into a convincing presentation for administration. These efforts have the potential to touch many patients' lives exponentially if certain improvements are agreed upon. When positive change is made, those involved get a taste of greater job satisfaction and the original frustrations will fade. The short term pain can yield long term gain for many. The Caring is the burning furnace inside, ever fueling and driving the momentum.

HELP WITH TIME MANAGEMENT

The time to relax is when you

don't have time for it.

Sydney J. Harris [2]

Even the most seasoned nurse has room for improvement in her time management. She can start by tracking her activities for one or two weeks on an appointment calendar, by writing down her activities during her waking hours on the calendar as she goes along her daily routines. After two weeks, the nurse has a lot of important data to examine. Viewing the results, she can see where there are productive things consistently happening and where there are gaps, spans of time spent inappropriately, and room for improvement.

MY OWN TIME TRACKING

I thought my time management would appear as a confusing mess. When I looked at my data, I found it was more like a symphony of job duties, schoolwork, housework, shopping, laundry, individual time with each child and my husband, time with the family collectively, church, relaxation, errands, gardening, and short visits with other family and friends. I discovered I needed to make more time for formal exercise aside from just gardening or short walks. I'm sure I cover countless miles while at work and when I am busy in daily activity, but that is not the same as intentional exercise. I found that what I managed best is the flow of the symphony of activity as I transition between all my areas of responsibility. What I managed poorly is the area of over-committing myself for work, as in projects or shift work. The other areas of my life are slighted because I don't say, "No!" as much as I should in my work activities.

I learned I must focus more on personal balance so there is more of "me" in each area of activity and that I needed to pay more attention to prioritizing so that the most important things are done first and last items can go into the next day or get postponed if necessary. Personal, spiritual, and emotional balance results in noticeable stress relief and creates a better "me" for the other areas of my life. It will also improve my mindset and attentiveness.

I learned I must focus more on personal

balance so there is more of "me" in

each area of activity.

COMPASSION FATIGUE

Webster defines fatigue as "physical or mental exhaustion; weariness." Compassion is defined as "sorrow for the sufferings or trouble of another or others, accompanied by the urge to help." [3] When we pollinate the two terms, we create a definition for compassion fatigue. Compassion fatigue is the physical or mental exhaustion or weariness resulting from sorrow for the sufferings of others, accompanied by the urge to help. People who work in healthcare, especially nurses, are required to show compassion routinely in their work and they easily can become overwhelmed by it. It is very common. If this sounds like you, you are not alone. If it is any consolation, we can remember that even Jesus had compassion fatigue. We see in the gospel of Matthew where He demonstrates it. Perhaps, compassion fatigue is yet another way we are to become like Christ, just as we share in many other types of His sufferings.

When he disembarked and saw the vast throng,

his heart was moved with pity

and He cured their sick.

Matthew 14:14

Again, before Jesus fed thousands of people, Matthew writes that Jesus called his disciples and said:

"My heart is moved with pity for the crowd.

By now they have been with me three days,

and have had nothing to eat.

I do not wish to send them away hungry,

for fear they may collapse along the way."

Matthew 15:32

WHAT ABOUT THE CHILDREN?

My first encounter with compassion fatigue happened when I was only sixteen years of age. I was in the city of Belem in Brazil as an exchange student for the summer. My inquisitive eyes devoured observations all over the city and within the home where I was a welcomed guest. My heart was pierced by many shocking sites. Everywhere I looked, I saw suffering. I often saw handicapped people struggling to function without appropriate equipment or prosthetics. The saddest site of all was that of the young children climbing around in huge garbage heaps in their bare feet and poorly clad bodies, looking for food and anything else that might be useful.

Any contribution to the greater good is

a contribution to all of humanity everywhere,

past, present, and future.

My ears were pierced by some of the saddest sounds I have ever known. I slept under a window on the second floor of the house. Peering through the window behind the home there was a vast, slum (favela) where hungry, sick children could be heard crying at all hours of the night. They lived in shacks comprised of layered trash. Most had no electricity or water. It was on one of these nights that my visiting, international mind decided to make a commitment to act at the local level back home. I grew increasingly determined to contribute at home, knowing that through our interconnectedness I could somehow contribute across the miles to the Latin world. Any contribution to the greater good is a contribution to all of humanity everywhere, past, present, and future.

When I returned home to my nursing assistant work and to finish high school, I met a Portuguese-speaking resident at the nursing home. I was able to converse with her because I had learned some Portuguese in Brazil. No one else in the facility could communicate with her. My local work had begun! I pursued my nursing studies with great dedication, inspired by the sites and sounds of Brazil. The rest of my nursing career continued to be embellished with examples of an international thinker acting locally. I still plan to continue to act locally with the things I have learned from the grand scheme which includes promoting diversity in all my dealings. I encourage all my colleagues to embrace diversity, to consider learning a second language, and to avoid ethnocentrism. All the countries and the cultures of the world are interconnected economically, socially, religiously, and through scholarship. The people of these places arrive in our local healthcare systems regularly. American nurses must be prepared.

I encourage all my colleagues to embrace

diversity, to consider learning a second

language, and to avoid ethnocentrism.

SELF-REFLECTION

It is good for nurses to make a habit of practicing personal quality improvement efforts. As we continually self-reflect on our personal growth, our teaching, our leading, and our professional duties, we are able to constantly improve. Evaluations can help with self-improvement, too. When there is constructive criticism, it is an opportunity for further growth and improvement. We figure out a plan of change and see if it helps. The Air Force teaches that a nurse can never stagnate. The military system really keeps nurses growing through cross-training and all kinds of maneuvers and training. An annual evaluation sets you on a course for another year of self improvement, step by step. A nurse with this experience arrives at her next evaluation as better officer and practitioner.

A nurse can never stagnate.

Nurses can take other actions to ensure vitality and growth. They can become more avid readers. Just as we need to get enough physical exercise, nurses must challenge themselves to mental gyrations as well. We need to be hooked on learning as life-long learners. Nurses also ensure vitality and growth by establishing more collegial relationships with colleagues that have high expectations for themselves. The right colleagues can help keep us growing and challenged and such benefits can be reciprocal between parties.

QUIET TIME

We need to find God, and He cannot

be found in noise and restlessness.

God is the friend of silence…The more we receive

in silent prayer, the more we can give in our active life.

We need silence to be able to touch souls.

Mother Teresa of Calcutta

The regular practice of having some quiet time to pray, relax the mind, and recharge the batteries is a good habit for de-stressing and preventing compassion fatigue.

Come to me, all you who are weary

and find life burdensome,

and I will refresh you.

Matthew 11:28

When Pope Benedict XVI was visiting in New York, he stated, "What matters most is that you develop your personal relationship with God. That relationship is expressed in prayer. God, by his very nature, speaks, hears, and replies." He goes on to mention that Paul urges the Thessalonians and us to pray constantly in the New Testament.[4]

Stress robs us of the contentment of constant prayer. It causes a chemical cascade in the body which must be halted, not perpetuated, if we want to be healthy. Some nurses use their commute time for de-stressing. Some do it with walking, or by taking in an intentional quiet time in a quiet spot. We have to recognize when the tension mounts in us. We have to recognize when it's time for a moment of rejuvenation. This is what Jesus Himself did. We see where He would withdraw to a garden or a mountain to pray. After He had walked on the water, Matthew writes that:

…He went up to the mountain by himself

to pray remaining there alone

as evening drew on.

Matthew 14:23-24

Sometimes Jesus spent the whole night in prayer:

He went out to the mountain to pray,

spending the whole night with God.

Luke 6:12

James also encourages us to pray:

Draw close to God, and

He will draw close to you.

James 4:8

God is the ultimate and original Source of power and strength. We can draw from Him to sustain us. He fills our cup so we can consistently share His love with our spouse, our children, our neighbors, co-workers, and patients each day. If a nurse routinely seeks refreshment and renewal for continuing in her work from the original Source of Caring, the Caring is abundant and limitless.

Draw your strength from the Lord

and his mighty power.

Ephesians 6:10

Peter urges us to:

Cast all your cares on him

because he cares for you.

1 Peter 5:7

We are also told to:

Be still, and know that I am God.

Psalm 46:10

DAY'S END

I took a walk along the lonesome shore,
And wondered if my day had taught me some
New thing. Perhaps a lesson learned, or more
Perhaps a memory to me has come.

The quiet night was slowly coming near,
The sun was softly resting o'er the sea.
The waves, I see, do hit the rocks and pier,
And there the shadows hit the ground and flee
Of gulls that soar with wings spread far and wide.

The end of day approached the quiet sands.
The silver moon got higher with the tide,
But disappeared for those in other lands.

The sun, I know, again will reappear,
And to reflect again I will be here.

Chris Feist Heilmeier at age 16

DUTY TO SELF

The American Nurses' Association (ANA) Code of Ethics has nine tenets. One of these tenets is especially difficult to support in the practice setting. This Fifth Tenet States, "The nurse owes the same duties to self as to others, including the responsibility to preserve integrity and safety, to maintain competence, and to continue personal and professional growth." [5] This means that the nurse must put as much effort into dutifully caring for herself and upholding herself in consistent, moral character as she does for the efforts she invests in her patients. This is something a nurse should be striving for throughout her career. There is always room for improvement. We know nurses tend to be very dedicated, devoted, and other-serving, which are admirable qualities and virtues. They seem as innate for the nurse toward the patient as a mother toward her child. How many nurses do you see direct as many efforts toward themselves and each other as they do for their patients?

Nurses experience a variety of emotions in their daily work or when transitioning to a new position ranging from feeling challenged, stimulated, overwhelmed, anxious, and frustrated to feeling competent, confident, and rewarded. Nurses can use many strategies when coping with daily stress and strain or when transitioning to a new role.

1. Strive to communicate well at all levels;
2. Try to be as non-threatening as possible in all dealings;
3. Develop a consistent reputation of being approachable;
4. Maintain a routine of regular exercise and good nutrition;
5. Continue in faith practices which provide a steady focus and centering;
6. Take advantage of the mentors or preceptors provided; and
7. Participate in hobbies for recreation;

If a nurse is seeking ways to develop and grow, she can take many actions to contribute to her development. She may take greater interest in the mission and activities of the organization to which she belongs, which always needs better-informed and effective members. When a nurse understands the mission and vision of her organization, she can see if her values and actions correspond. The nurse can use this familiarity with the mission and vision of her organization to inspire and teach the less-involved members. She networks for the purpose of teaching and to make the desire for life-long learning contagious. She becomes a positive force of optimism.

> The main reason professionals join
>
> associations is to be able to
>
> network and share information. [6]

A growing nurse may want to pursue interaction and camaraderie with other nurses she wants to emulate. Colleagues network not only to teach, but to learn. The main reason professionals join associations is to network and share information.[6] A developing nurse may even want to seek out scholarly individuals in the other professional disciplines in healthcare to gain a greater understanding of their concerns and issues. She can learn the perspective of the dietician, therapists, physicians, and more. She may join a healthcare organization which includes a variety of disciplines so that the context of issues considered is expanded.[7] A nurse leader or educator who is seen as an individual who understands others' perspectives will be more effective and better received by the members. Such networking promotes effective change.

LIFE-LONG LEARNING

Professional development and further education changes us as human beings. We are better informed and equipped as nurse clinicians, nurse leaders, and nurse educators. These abilities, confidences, and competencies cross over into the other areas of life.

They are all integrated. Becoming a scholar gives a new way to look at life in general and not nursing specifically. Students in every area of study need to be well-read in a variety of topics, which is especially true of nurses. Nurses can contribute to their lifelong learning process by being well-read in many topics. Professional development and further education both give nurses greater credibility. The well-informed nurse can substantiate her opinions and views better by using convincing knowledge, research, and experience.

Self development helps a nurse grow satisfied with the person she has become. She gives back to the community she lives in. It is more than just making a salary. Rather, it is part of "the calling" to be a nurse. The salary is just for sustaining her to be able to continue to serve. She distributes her Caring throughout all duties, appreciating all individuals with dignity and respect, promoting everyone's educational advancement, and challenging everyone to address their own spirituality.

WHO IS IN CHARGE?

When circumstances seem insurmountable, the nurse of faith can remind herself Who is really in charge. We remind ourselves that God has everything under His control and He is never late. It takes blind faith and trust sometimes, but God always pulls through for us. Eventually, we understand each dilemma, sometimes years later.

We know that God makes all things work

together for the good of those who have

been called according to his decree.

Romans 8:28

A NURSING STUDENT STRUGGLES
I once met a nursing student who was struggling with the pressures and demands of her studies. I could see that

the stress of school was taking a big toll on her. Wanting to help, I asked her, "Tina, do you think God wants you to be a nurse?" She answered, "Yes, I believe He does." I replied, "Then don't you think it's His job to help you through this? You do your part and trust Him to do His." She was very relieved and peace came over her. She just needed to be reminded that He was supporting her learning process.

Is it possible that He who did not spare His own Son

but handed Him over for the sake of us all

will not grant us all things besides?

Romans 8:32

NURTURING SELF TO CARE MORE

The elderly need and will need advocates, especially with the dynamic of our ageing Boomers. Every nurse should have at least one foot entrenched in gerontology. A majority of our patients are elders. The need for dementia education and awareness is dramatic. In our communities, many of our elders are at risk for abuse or neglect because families do not understand dementia. Nurses must do all they can to educate the public in dementia and they need to be inspirational as leaders and educators, whether they are helping elderly patients, family members, colleagues, students, or community members. The nurse carries the caring, intellectual, and interpersonal expertise into all facets of life. These aspects are not confined to the workplace but extend into all relationships, especially toward loved ones and community members. Nurses need to be careful enough to keep on caring, both at work and beyond.

GROWING IN THE KNOWLEDGE OF DISASTER MANAGEMENT

There is a recent growing need for healthcare workers to be educated in disaster preparedness. In light of recent violence and disasters, more healthcare resource dollars are being directed toward preparedness.[8] It is important for nurses to be knowledgeable in disaster processes, especially for our weak and vulnerable patients and residents. The public requires better awareness of our elders' needs in disaster situations. This is an area of interest where some nurses may find much purpose and fulfillment.

CERTIFICATION

Specialty certifications make a positive difference for nurses, patients, the profession, and organizations in many ways. A large survey of certified nurses showed that: "51 percent reported greater confidence in their practice, 35 percent felt greater confidence in their decision-making ability, 28 percent reported more confidence in their ability to detect complications, 23 percent reported more effective communication and collaboration with other health care providers, and 6 percent reported fewer adverse events and errors in patient care than before they were certified."[9] This is very good news. Who would have ever guessed that so many positives could come from a nursing certification? This study proves the worth of certifications.

THE NURSE'S PORTFOLIO

It is always a good idea to maintain a career portfolio. One nice advantage of developing a portfolio is being able to consolidate one's career information in one location, making it complete and easily accessible. One concern is all the effort it takes to maintain it and keep it current. A portfolio helps a future healthcare leader by providing a career roadmap, showing where one has been, and includes her strengths, weaker areas, and gaps. A portfolio indicates where growth and exploration should expand and a strong portfolio could mean the difference between getting a highly competitive job or not. Boosting a portfolio can impact a nurse's professional health.

SOLIDARITY WITH SUFFERING

One nurse leader, Dr. Stanford-Blair, spent a lot of time and effort studying leaders in a scholarly, measurable, and scientific manner. What she discovered from observing all these admirable leaders was that they had several self-sustaining behaviors in common. One of the self-sustaining behaviors she promotes is to "welcome inspiration through connection to a higher purpose." [10] We connect to our higher purpose (God) through prayer and we receive refreshment.

How many of our brothers and sisters all over the world, end up at this connection to a higher purpose (which is God) who do *not* have good education, health, emotional stability, money resources, or even enough food. The universal destination seems to always be God. People have higher-order needs met, as in their connection to God, even though lower order needs are not always met. This seems to contradict Maslow's Hierarchy of Needs. That is what I have always loved about the sufferers in places like the third world, hospital beds, hospice, counseling, therapy, and addictions treatment centers. There's a solidarity amongst those who suffer that often surpasses power and money and success. It puts sufferers all on the same playing field.

...God of all consolation. He comforts us in all our

afflictions and thus enables us to comfort those

who are in trouble, with the same

consolation we have received from Him.

2 Corinthians 1:3-4

Have you ever noticed how folks who *have* suffered have concern and pray for those who *are* suffering? Some even identify with the One who suffered, too, carrying their crosses. I am grateful that some people are able to somehow draw strength from this solidarity of suffering. It worked for me. Years ago, I went through a painful divorce. I didn't know where to start to heal or that it was even possible to heal at all. Nothing worked until I started to meditate on other peoples' suffering, especially the Passion of the One (years before the movie came out). It was only then that I started to heal. That was a long time ago, but it still helps me even today to have compassion for those who are struggling or suffering in life.

Those things that hurt instruct.

Benjamin Franklin

Paul talks about suffering in his writings to the Colossians, too:

Even now I find my joy in the suffering

I endure for you.

In my own flesh I fill up what is lacking

in the sufferings of Christ

for the sake of his body, the church.

Colossians 1:24

HUMOR HELPS

At the opposite side of the spectrum, nurses can easily see the value of humor in healthcare to boost a colleague's spirits. We could write volumes on the funniest events we have seen in healthcare.

PETRIFYING PROLAPSES

When I was just a naïve teen working as a nursing assistant, I happened upon some shocking surprises while doing evening care on a couple of residents. I thought we needed to call an ambulance urgently the first evening I was washing Eva. Right there, plain as could be, sat her bladder, outside her body!! "Oh my, oh my!" I said, "Eva, Eva, what should I do? What is this? Should we call the ambulance?" She replied in her classic Pennsylvania Dutch accent, "Oh, no, that's just my bladder." Palpating it, I said, "I thought it was supposed to be on the inside of your body. Does it hurt you?" She replied, "No, no, it's been that way for years." I was mortified.

In another instance, Sweet Verna sat perched on the toilet. She rang the call bell for assistance. I approached, only to find another petrifying situation for a naïve teen. Verna stated, "Chris, can you get the nurse because my rectum fell out." I was mortified. "I ran to the nurse, "Judy, Judy! Verna's rectum fell out! What should we do? Should we get the ambulance to come?" Judy calmly replied, "I'll just put it back." I exclaimed, "What? You're just gonna put it back? Don't you need surgery or something for fixing this?" Judy answered, "No, it happens all the time." It was mortified yet again by yet another petrifying prolapse.

A SURPRISE DEMONSTRATION

On another occasion, I was working an evening shift as a nursing assistant. It was the middle of supper. Residents were stationed throughout the dining room in geri-chairs and wheelchairs for their meal. One woman suffered a completely blocked airway and became unresponsive. We feverishly worked to remove the obstruction, right there in full view of all the residents dining.

Fortunately, we were able to restore her respirations. Her color quickly returned, and the staff was greatly relieved. One inquisitive resident stood at the entrance to the dining room and asked in a sophisticated voice, "Is this a demonstration?" We broke into laughter at the thought of this intense event being misconstrued as intentional dining entertainment.

TRICKS OF THE TUBES

It was late one night. I was the nurse for a dear elderly man with a recent hip repair. He got pleasantly confused as the night drew on. Instead of sleeping, he decided to get busy. There was a lot to do in that solitary bed of his. He had all kinds of interesting things with him that he could experiment with. He had a foley, a hip dressing, and some plastic socks (compression boots) on his legs that squeezed his legs off and on. What fun.

I entered his room to check on him, and found the funniest site of my career. This creative man was humming in his bed, making inventions with his gismos. Somehow, he was able to successfully connect his compression boot motor to his foley bag. He watched as the foley bag inflated and deflated at predictable intervals. He was entertained and so was I. It was the funniest site I have ever seen.

CHAPTER TEN

CELEBRATING THE SAGES

—⟨☉⟩

I am sure of this much:

that He who has begun the good work in you

will carry it through to completion,

right up to the day of Christ Jesus.

Philippians 1:6

AGEING NURSES

The Robert Wood Johnson Foundation deserves much credit for its thorough study of the demographics and trends impacting Nursing today. The foundation published a study in 2006 titled: *Wisdom at Work: the Importance of the Older and Experienced Nurse in the Workplace*. This 73 page report reveals the high cost of losing older nurses. It supplies worthwhile recommendations and conclusions for the reader. Any healthcare leader would be very wise to heed the advice of this report. The proper actions taken now can help avoid future, expensive issues and losses in Nursing.

The Johnson report explains that we have an ageing population in our country which is growing larger, while simultaneously, fewer people are entering Nursing and staying there. It is estimated that by the year 2010, 40 percent of the entire nursing workforce will be over the age of 50.[1] This information is staggering. From this fact, we can draw the conclusion that 40 percent of nurses are Baby Boomers themselves! The report also explains how expensive it is to for healthcare facilities to endure high turnover of nurses. A survey of hospitals (acute care) showed that as a rule, the replacement cost of a nurse is equal to or greater than two times the nurse's annual salary. Recruiting, hiring, and training expenses add up quickly. For example, a medical-surgical nurse making $50,000 per year would cost the facility $100,000 or more to replace. To replace a specialty nurse is even more expensive for the institution. Older workers with greater longevity tend to have lower turnover, which offsets the expense of the younger workers with higher turnover.[2]

The report also sites studies which dispel many myths about older workers. These studies show that a majority of older workers *want* to be learning new things in their work. Any possible physical limitations the older worker may have are usually far outweighed by their knowledge, experience, and well-developed interpersonal skills. An older worker is often more capable of identifying a break-through in an organization because of his/her cumulative wisdom.

SUGGESTED PROGRAMS

The report highlights suggestions for organizations to help retain or attract older workers. Some of these include:

o Alternative roles
o A health benefit option for part-time employees
o Mentoring programs between experienced and newer employees
o Phased retirement options
o Post-retirement rehiring options
o Informative injury prevention programs

o   Availability of rehabilitation programs and physical therapy on-site
o   Career growth training
o   Paid additional time off for caregiving and caregiving leave options
o   Special features for older workers in the Employee Assistance Program
o   Retiree health benefits
o   Long-term care insurance with employer subsidy or group purchase option
o   On-site fitness and wellness programs
o   Assistance with individualized retirement preparation [3]

ERGONOMIC CONCERNS

According to the studies sited in this report, some of the older nurses' ergonomic concerns include the extent of the workload, floating, re-assignment, the different perception of staffing between staff nurses and administration, shortages of the nurses' support personnel, the need for state mandated staffing levels, minimal staff and support at night, and a lack of a process to support staffing when acuity escalates during a shift. Some practical ergonomic solutions are given in the study. Some of these improvements include:

o   Reducing distances nurses have to walk by making supplies more accessible in a variety of locations
o   Workplace designs to include decentralized nursing stations and accommodations for optimal safety
o   Over bed lifts for increasing numbers of obese patients
o   Adjustable lighting options
o   Readily accessible accommodations for nurses' personal needs
o   Adequate storage and workspace areas to reduce clutter
o   Adequate storage space for equipment necessary for patient care
o   Consistent, standardized design of patient rooms

o Careful decoration considerations to enhance the work environment

o Acoustic design to eliminate hazards of noise [4]

STRATEGIES OF THE HEART

Multiple authors and studies mentioned in the report uncover the older worker's appreciation of respect and trust in the workplace. A variety of suggestions are given for enhancing the older workers job satisfaction:

o Provide adequate time for renewal like breaks and time off

o Offer services that enhance time off like elder care or laundry services

o Move to more principle-centered policies and procedures rather than rigid ones

o Promote managerial respect for all workers including openness to inclusive decision-making and sharing credit where due

o Choose passionate, compassionate, competent, honest and ethical managers

o Promote increased feedback mechanisms

o Emphasize the mission cause, not the business, to match the workers' own values

o Honor all the spiritual aspects of health care work and workers

o Promote all varieties of staff development

o Promote new technologies that lighten the work load rather than expand it [5]

We do not lose heart,

because our inner being is renewed each day

even though our body is being destroyed

at the same time.

2 Corinthians 4:16-18

USING THE INTELLECTUAL CAPITAL

The report sites one study where a significant number of career nurses between the ages of 45 and 64 were interviewed. What was discovered was the treasure of talents these sages possess. These individuals tend to possess excellent, analytical problem-solving skills, a remarkable ability to navigate the system to create change in healthcare, a good understanding of patient flow, ability to provide extraordinary patient-centered care, significant professional authority, and well-developed intuitive skills as a result of experience and education.

The sages believed it is important to differentiate between the older, expert nurse who possesses decades of experience in patient-centered care and the novice, second-career nurse who was older but lacks the experience and expertise. The sages believe senior nurses have much to contribute because of certain characteristics they share. They are calm during emergencies and promote calmness in the atmosphere of one. They are accomplished, dedicated, and experienced. They are committed to the profession more than profit, hard-working, knowledgeable, intuitive, and accomplished in decision-making. They are dedicated team players and they carry a "been there, done that" attitude.[6]

For the Lord gives wisdom,

from His mouth come knowledge and understanding;

He has counsel in store for the upright,

He is the shield of those who walk uprightly.

Proverbs 2:6-7

The sages identify the barriers that make it most difficult to continue practicing their expertise at the bedside. They are all related to the physical demands of the work. Some examples include lack or inconsistent use of patient lifting devices and other technologies, centralized workstations, long hallways, high patient census, and challenging work schedules. It is no wonder that senior nurses cross over to less strenuous positions in nursing or healthcare. Thus, much of the bedside brainpower is lost. Through mentoring, the wisdom and knowledge of the older nurses are passed to the next generation. Consequently, the nurses and their patients would be severely hurt if these senior, knowledgeable, experienced nurses would suddenly leave the healthcare system.[7]

Let endurance come to its perfection

so that you may be fully mature

and lacking in nothing.

James 1:4

INNOVATIVE AND CREATIVE ROLES FOR THE AGING NURSE

With all these desirable attributes of older nurses identified, healthcare organizations are wise to find ways to use the intellectual capital these nurses possess. The best way to expand the superior knowledge and skills of these nurses exponentially is through a variety of roles involving the sage and the novice. These roles could include coaching individuals, coaching teams, precepting, educating in staff development, and working as a safety officer, diversity trainer, community liaison, relief nurse, patient educator, family advocate, or a quality coach.[8]

REVIEW OF RECOMMENDED BEST PRACTICES

Fear of the Lord is the beginning of knowledge.

Proverbs 1:7

The Johnson report also summarizes the recommended actions organizations can take to maximize knowledge transfer and manage talent well. One worthwhile habit for any healthcare organization to take to recruit and retain older nurses is to be aware of the best practices recommended for doing so. This is an ongoing process. Assessing for and correcting administrative misperceptions about recruiting and retaining older nurses are ongoing actions which could be put into practice. An organization might consider creating new, attractive programs like portable pensions and phased retirements, to attract and keep older nurses. Regular assessments of the work environment can be done to uncover the issues affecting nurses' intent to stay or not. These can then be addressed once they are identified.[9]

Ergonomic and design changes to accommodate the older nurse are advised. Continuing education for seasoned nurses can be customized so they can stay challenged throughout their careers. Older nurses can transition into new, creative roles that help improve patient care like mentoring and coaching. These are great ways to manage and expand the talents and skills of the seasoned nurses. They mix their activity with the work of the newer nurses, enhancing the transfer of knowledge and skill.[10]

Organizations are wise to remain aware of the draws that help to retain senior nurses and act accordingly. Senior nurses prefer a supportive workplace where they are invited to participate in the decision-making, receive recognition and positive feedback, and socially interact with patients and colleagues. They prefer less strenuous jobs that are safe, effective, and ergonomically friendly. They want favorable schedules and they like having more control over the workplace. They want to expand their talents into new, creative roles. They will consider retirement programs which make it attractive to work longer. Any proactive organization is acutely aware of the high cost of losing their intellectual capital and will take actions to preserve it.[11] Healthcare must do all it can to keep these experienced nurses active in the workplace. It can't afford not to.

Do you not know or have you not heard?

The Lord is the eternal God,

Creator of the ends of the earth.

He does not faint nor grow weary,

And his knowledge is beyond scrutiny.

He gives strength to the fainting;

For the weak He makes vigor abound.

Though young men faint and grow weary,

And youths stagger and fall,

They that hope in the Lord will renew their strength,

They will soar as with eagles' wings;

They will run and not grow weary,

Walk and not grow faint.

Isaiah 40:28-31

CHAPTER ELEVEN

LEADERSHIP

Nothing is so strong as gentleness,

nothing is so gentle as real strength.

St. Francis De Sales [1]

Having worked in a variety of hospitals and nursing homes has given me a broad idea of how many leaders operate in healthcare. I have had many opportunities to observe both strong and weak leadership in action. All the effective leaders I have ever had the opportunity to observe have had similar attributes and core values. These core values include integrity, fairness, forgiveness, morality, and respect and love for God and others. Effective, true leaders are few and far between. The very best leaders I have ever seen were without a doubt found in the United States Air Force, on both the enlisted and officer sides of the service. Seeing someone motivate and mobilize individuals and groups is a wondrous and magical process to witness. True leadership becomes tangible and measurable when we examine and study the attributes of excellent leaders.

Seeing someone motivate and mobilize

individuals and groups is a wondrous

and magical process to witness.

DIGNITY AND ESTEEM FOR ALL

One attribute effective healthcare leaders have in common is their ongoing respect and appreciation for each and every follower. The purpose of a leader is to direct and move the activity of others successfully. This requires an ability to motivate others toward movement and change. We know humans tend to resist change. Maybe healthcare workers fear and resist change because of the difficult and unpleasant experiences they have had to endure in the past. Many function under bosses that do not have enough resources and/or leadership abilities. Some individuals in positions of authority lack social skills and some are outright anti-social. Even the workers and nurses with least seniority exhibit a perceptive awareness of the weaknesses and flaws of those above them in their chain of command. Employees want progress on one hand, yet on the other hand they want to protect themselves from living same common, unpleasant, painful experiences which tend to roll down upon them. It is like they are in a state of collective post-traumatic stress from their history of undignified treatment and neglect as employees. When we look at the overall masses of front-line healthcare workers, we see the same leadership mistakes play over and over in different places. A wise, perceptive employee with any stretch of longevity can begin to feel like he/she is living the same miserable Groundhog Day over and over, reliving the mismanagement and mistreatment repetitively: same neglect, different boss. Many times the older and wiser employees at the bottom of the food chain actually carry those in authority by their quiet, obedient example, prayers, and dedicated work style. This is the good fruit we see in the work of a devoted, faith-based nurse or healthcare employee.

In everything you do,

act without grumbling or arguing.

Philippians 2:14

Every leadership mishap in every field can be traced back to poor communication. Staff members resist progress and efforts of those in authority because they feel marginalized, uninformed, trampled over, and unappreciated. They comment to each other, "Let's sit back and watch this new idea fail. It will never work. It's never been that way here." Other thoughts shared between employees sound like, "It won't be long before this boss, manager, or director is fired or quits. Things will stay the same in the end. They'll never get anywhere." A "we" and "they" mentality develops, subdividing the organization into pockets. This is very detrimental to an organization's attempts at forward progress.

In the end, all business operations can be

reduced to three words: people, product

and profits. People come first.

Lee Iacocca [2]

Wise healthcare leaders present a new process from the employees' perspective and demonstrate how it will help them. It is very safe to involve lower-level workers in decision-making. This is very unattractive to most leaders because they perceive they will be losing power. Negativity toward a change process can be completely averted if workers are empowered and time and effort are taken to introduce the idea to the employees carefully. This is nothing short of good communication. Employees will trust the word of a leader who has a loyal track record with them. Their buy-in guarantees the success of the change effort. We learn from our military folks that if you take good care of your troops, they will take care of you and make you look good!

Every individual in every organization is an integral part of the team. The leaders must treat them as such. How many nurse leaders know the name of the housekeeper in the workplace? How about the dietary folks? Or someone from maintenance? Frontline health-care workers know there are few leaders who go out consistently to greet and appreciate them. Some have <u>never</u> had this type of boss or leader. Many leaders are perceived by the frontline as hiding or residing in their ivory tower, spewing mandates. This is not the operating procedure that Christ suggests for those in authority. The Bible is clear on how to lead and esteem others.

Let the greater among you be as the junior,

the leader as the servant.

Who in fact is greater-

he who reclines at table or he

who serves the meal?

Luke 22:26-27

An excellent nurse leader gains respect and loyalty when she puts herself at the service of her subordinates. The employees see her act fairly and advocate for them. In return, she gains their loyalty. She could be away for a month and they'll keep the work-place running well in her absence. A true nurse leader knows that she is in the service of others. Once a leader has the trust of the employees, the front line will be more apt to accept change. The nurse leader needs to constantly question traditional management practices and promote the welfare of her troops. She knows how to win their loyalty and inspire them to embrace positive change. Any leader capable of making a significant impression is one who advocates for her followers. Respect, appreciation, fairness, and integrity are all part of this mix. Only then can new changes succeed.

Anyone among you who aspires to greatness

must serve the rest,

and whoever wants to rank first among you

must serve the needs of all.

Matthew 20:26-27

THE HEALTHCARE WORKERS' DAILY PRAYER

Please join your co-workers in this Workers' Daily Prayer to unite us as believers in this healthcare organization and call down God's protection and blessing upon our workplace.

Dear Lord, we know You deserve all the credit for any of our success at work or at home. We ask you to help us remember everyone's dignity as we do our daily work. Please bless the work of our hands and make it holy. Please protect our workplace from all evil, and guide all our leaders in their actions and decisions. Give our leaders the wisdom and insight they need to create a workplace that shows respect for every patient, every worker. Help us to find Your way in the middle of our burdens, and give us the strength we need to carry our load as if we were doing it for You. We know you once carried a heavy cross for us and we thank you for the hope and life Your cross gives us. Amen.

(Please feel free to copy and distribute this prayer to workers of faith in your organization.)

155

AN EMPHASIS ON APPRECIATION

We can be sure that a healthcare leader is a humble, thankful person if she is careful enough to show sincere appreciation to her staff routinely. A thankful person is always a humble, happy person. Thankfulness puts the focus outside of self to where blessings come from. It is an act of pride for us to even consider ourselves humble. Humility, happiness, and thankfulness are all directly related.

I will give thanks to you, O Lord,

with all my heart;

I will declare all your wondrous deeds.

Psalm 9:1-2

COMMUNICATION

Excellent leaders master the ability to communicate and convey information to employees from the employees' vantage point. Communication is a means of informing another through words, actions, attitudes, body language, and behavior. Ideas are conveyed so individuals or groups can be motivated to embrace their work. They are more likely to take ownership of their workload if they understand how it contributes to the effort as a whole. A great leader knows how to convey information well.

Life is not so short but that there is

always time enough for courtesy.

Emerson [3]

Well-developed communication is a key leadership attribute because it is the translation of one's ideas, goals, and expectations as a leader to the team so that goals can be accomplished together.[4]

The capacity of the leader is compounded and multiplied when it is synergized through activity with other individuals. If a nurse leader becomes a better communicator, then she will subsequently become a better leader. There is an improvement made to the organization and profession of Nursing as a whole.

Well-developed communication

is a key leadership attribute

because it is the translation of one's ideas,

goals and expectations as a leader to the team

so that goals can be accomplished together.[4]

All the ways a faith-filled nurse leader communicates to others must be consistent, as these ways reflect her personal values. Co-workers should not have to ask each other, "Is she in a bad mood today?" or "Is it a good day for this?" It is difficult to remain consistent in good communication when other factors and stressors continuously enter daily life. This is where the great leaders are able to sort and prioritize issues while maintaining their composure and ability to lead.

Communication improves with practice and usage. It is also enhanced when the communicator maintains a mentality of abundance, always keeping an optimistic attitude, and always noting that there will be enough people, resources, creativity, and determination to accomplish anything together. Faith-filled nurse leaders are sure of this because they place themselves transparently before God every day, making Him the most important force in the mix, knowing that their very next breath is in His hands.

It is not that we are entitled of ourselves

to take credit for anything.

Our sole credit is from God.

2 Corinthians 3:5

Good communication has to start at the top and must flow both vertically and horizontally. What consequences result from a lack of ability to convey information? The results include poor customer satisfaction and poor delivery of care due to delay of resources and services. It also produces irate families, fluctuating and inconsistent morale of employees, poor staff retention, and endless staffing difficulties. Staff members need to be informed of what to expect so they can begin preparations when possible. When a multi-faceted system comes together and performs well to achieve a goal or surpass a challenge, the members feel like together they have created magic. They especially like when the right hand knows what the left is doing.

Improved communication is a great start for enhancing any organization. It happens verbally, non-verbally, in writing, and electronically. It is *the most* powerful tool for empowerment and growth. Networking with multiple other individuals creates more pathways for greater information transport. An effective leader knows to network heavily- both vertically and horizontally- to glean and share valuable information. She learns who is capable of what, and can direct activity accordingly.

Once better communication is established, the visionary leaders can plan the work, communicate it to the employees, and together they can work the plan. All areas can then move forward. Visionary leaders not only generate the vision, but are inspirational enough communicators to package it, sell it, and orchestrate it. They are able to carry out the steps by empowering others. The vision is realized by motivating and empowering facets of the organization step by step. Not only are the followers being led, but the flow and timing of the change is being carefully maneuvered. The organization becomes like a strategic chess match where certain pieces capable of certain maneuvers are carefully positioned and activated with cautious timing and patience. Communication is the most critical, essential element in the process of actualizing a vision because it is the catalyst for activating individuals and groups.

Communication is the most critical,

essential element in the

process of actualizing a vision.

Once goals are clearly communicated, appropriate individuals and sections of an organization can be empowered to accomplish each of their contributing actions. How can a leader build upon the strengths and talents of individual members? They start by esteeming *every* individual in an organization as a valuable contributor and facilitate their growth. They maintain a fair and consistent approach with each person and promote a regular system of appreciation and recognition. Members are rewarded appropriately through praise, monetary compensation, promotions, benefits, and awards.

They start by esteeming *every* individual

in an organization as a valuable contributor.

The excellent nurse leader fosters the unique and diverse combination of qualities, attributes and characteristics of the individual employees. She draws out dormant talents and potentials that come to life and recreate the members. She has confidence in her troops. The end result is an improving, evolving, living, thriving organization.

The excellent nurse leader is more concerned with the successes of her subordinates than with her own successes. She removes their barriers and gently provides the fertilizer and nurturing they need to grow both personally and in their work activities. The individuals flourish without being overly controlled or micromanaged. She encourages her staff members to be good to each other and support each other with a "go girl" spirit. She knows that people need to be good to each other. Members celebrate each other's successes. As employees experience positive growth, the organization has better morale, becomes more efficient and improves the delivery of care. The end result is better patient care because employees are treated well and flourish.

The excellent nurse leader is more concerned

with the successes of her subordinates

than with her own successes.

MENTORING AND GROOMING

Being able to mentor well is a key leadership attribute because it is a way to pass the torch, educate, and teach future leaders this practice of good leadership. The art and science of leadership would disappear if mentors ceased to convey it to others. Mentoring develops and renews followers. If a nurse leader demonstrates her ethical core values, they are likely to be noticed and practiced by others [6] as in setting an example. Good mentoring helps the mentor and the follower improve. Thus, a collective improvement of the group and profession as a whole is created.

The art and science of leadership

would disappear

if mentors ceased to convey it to others.

Mentoring that is consistent with personal values can be demonstrated by the way the mentor treats the mentee. Fairness, integrity, and respect must be demonstrated consistently throughout the process. Then, the learner can duplicate the mentoring role in her own life. The impact spreads exponentially from there.

Mentoring has several strategies that belong under its umbrella: precepting, role modeling, coaching, networking, and sponsoring.[7] If a nurse is a parent, the most important mentoring role she possesses involves modeling for and teaching her children. Faith-filled parents today feel an urgency to teach their children how to think wisely and morally because they know they are not exposed to many appropriate role models in the world of media, sports, and music. They try to teach their children how to be good parents while they are still being parented. They want them to be prepared for the barrage of challenges that lie ahead, especially when they are no longer here on this earth. Life-coaching is the parents' job throughout, even when they are gone, because the legacy of what they have taught their children lives on after them.

Life-coaching is the parents' job throughout.

Aside from parenting, nurse leaders are often required to mentor, coach, and sponsor co-workers in addition to their normal duties. Strong nurse leaders are mindful of mentoring their novice colleagues such as nursing students and new nurses. They know this job is not to be taken lightly, and these nurse learners must not be viewed as a bother. The effective nurse sponsor realizes the novice employee is not an interruption, but a gift. She is placed in her path for a reason and the mentee is embraced as a treasure to be enhanced.

ESTEEMING THE ELDERS

Many leaders today fear that these young nurses have unimaginable challenges ahead. I once had a chance to speak briefly to 200+ nursing students at a college as a representative of long-term care (LTC). The most important idea I could conjure up to share with these wide-eyed novices was a simple plea. I asked them to please remember the elderly in their work. The elderly will need them to advocate for them. They may not think the long-term care field and gerontology are as glamorous as some of the other nursing specialties, but each is rewarding and very necessary in healthcare. Our society needs the awareness and dedication of all nurses, as the elderly are some of its weakest and most vulnerable members.

People who do not cherish their elderly have

forgotten whence they came

and whither they will go.

Ramsey Clark [8]

Jesus often encourages us to look after the widow and the orphan. Many believers fear that the welfare of the elderly in America and across the planet is likely to suffer tremendous insults over the next few decades. We see that natural resources are being perceived as growing scarce. Countries scramble like jackals at the kill for the resources our planet affords us. People of faith need to remind themselves that God tells us in Genesis to be fruitful and multiply. He wants us to subdue the earth and awards us dominion over the plants and animals. The Biblical world view remains very different from the contemporary world view. Something is terribly wrong in a world where the oil in the womb of Alaska has better protection than the child in the womb of his mother. Will our precious elderly be given the same label of "inconvenient" that too many of the unborn are stamped with? America, in her ignorance, might someday condone mixing the blood of our elderly with the blood of our unborn martyrs. May God have mercy on the souls responsible for our culture of death.

Something is terribly wrong in a world

where the oil in the womb of Alaska

has better protection than the child

in the womb of his mother.

While addressing a crowd in New York, Pope Benedict XVI speaks of repression of those who are most vulnerable:

"What happens when people, especially the most vulnerable, encounter a clenched fist of repression or manipulation rather than a hand of hope? ...drug and substance abuse, homelessness and poverty, racism, violence and degradation... While the causes of these problems are complex, all have in common a poisoned attitude of mind which results in people being treated as mere objects – a callousness of heart takes hold which first ignores, then ridicules the God-given identity of every human being. Such tragedies also point to what might have been and what could be were there other hands – your hands – reaching out. I encourage you to invite others, especially the vulnerable and the innocent, to join you along the way of goodness and hope."

Pope Benedict XVI [9]

Jesus knew we would always be challenged to help the widow, the orphan, the poor, and the disenfranchised all throughout every era in history. He knew this because he knew that greed would always be present. Jesus knew peoples' selfish, sinful nature very well. He was aware that the manna hoarded in the desert spoiled. Perhaps this is why He teaches us to humbly ask for our bread *daily*.

The Lord's Prayer

Our Father who art in heaven, hallowed be thy name. Thy kingdom come, thy will be done on earth, as it is in heaven. Give us this day our daily bread. And forgive us our debts, as we also forgive our debtors. And lead us not into temptation, but deliver us from evil.

Matthew 6:9-13

YOUR CARING FOOTPRINT

Today we are being taught by society to be careful about the impact of our carbon footprint on the planet. Do we have other footprints which impact our planet and society? Of course we do. Ask yourself if you would be re-elected into your position each year by the members of your organization.[10] What differences are you making? What kind of legacy are you leaving? Fifteen years from now, what improvements would you hope to be able to say you have made in your profession? Is your education furthered? Will you be known as a strong leader that was able to foster growth in your organization? Are you appreciating the unique and diverse combination of qualities, attributes, and characteristics of the employees? Are dormant talents and potentials coming to life to reshape your workplace?

You must shine among them like stars.

Philippians 2:15

Are you an educator who has been able to influence the next generation of nurses with clinical competence and reinforced the timeless ethics and principles in Nursing? Are you a patient preceptor? Are you encouraging the individuals in your organization to be good to each other and support each other with a "go girl" spirit of encouragement? Are you celebrating your colleagues' successes? Have you seen your workplace become more efficient with the overall delivery of care improving from your efforts? The growth possibilities are endless. Healthcare will never run out of opportunities for the motivated nurse to work her magic.

The future is worth expecting.

Henry David Thoreau

What abundant variety abounds in this world we call Nursing! Through this profession, we could never possibly exhaust the opportunities for new discovery of God, self, and others! Mother Nursing affords us a limitless supply of fulfillment, knowledge, enrichment, and growth, *unprecedented* by any other profession in history. Sometimes we, as nurses, touch lives deeply, sometimes our lives are deeply touched. Sometimes we lead individuals or groups, sometimes we follow strong leaders. Sometimes we give orders, sometimes we obey them. Many times we teach and much more often we learn. We even learn from our children, patients, students, and subordinates.

Our caring footprint leaves

a permanent imprint on peoples' hearts

and eternity as a whole.

Yes, we *are* being told to be careful about the impact of our carbon footprint on the planet. There might be some validity to that. We know that we must be good stewards of all that God gives us and that He expects more from those who have been given more. But our Caring Footprint, as nurses and believers, has a much broader and eternal effect than any carbon footprint could ever imagine. Our Caring Footprint leaves a permanent impression on peoples' hearts and eternity as a whole. When we look at all the selfless things that nurses do, it doesn't take much effort to see that nurses are truly sent from heaven to be instruments of God's healing and Caring right here on the face of the earth.

The harvest is good

But the workers are scarce.

Beg the harvest master to

Send out laborers to gather his harvest.

Matthew 9:37

THE LAST STORY

The last story is yet to be written because it is the description of what you will be doing next. As you go out and punch that clock or answer that call light or don those surgical scrubs or cry with that family or breathe with that woman or stop that bleeding or comfort that child or teach that lesson or change that dressing or insert that tube or present that idea of yours in the board room or give the bad news or volunteer to fill in a shift or feed that baby or make that phone call or travel to that disaster or write that evaluation or make that home visit or attend that funeral or give that medicine or help that inmate or go back to school or feed that elder or shock that chest or explain that procedure or calm that family. How will your story go? That is for you to decide. Will you remember to let Caring flow through those loving hands of yours? Every time you wash your hands, you have fifteen seconds to think about what those hands will be doing next. Choose to use them for Caring. I guarantee it will make a great story!

God does not ask your ability or inability.

He asks only your availability.

Mary Kay Ash [11]

Are you available to create a great story?

NOTE TO THE READER

If you would like to share a special, true caring story, or if you simply want to share a comment on this book, please write to me at: ShareMyStory@NursesAreFromHeaven.com. I would love to hear your story, whether it is from the patient's perspective or the nurse's. A web site is also available at: NursesAreFromHeaven.com. Please keep the faith. May God bless you in all you do and multiply the work of your holy hands.

In Him,
Chris

NOTES

Chapter 3

1. B. Phillips and M. Reagan, *The All-American Quote Book* (Eugene, OR: Harvest House, 1995), 50.

2. Ibid., 68.

3. M. E. Parker, *Nursing Theories and Nursing Practice* (Philadelphia: FA. Davis Company, 2001), 392-93.

4. A. Boykin (Speaker). Laureate Education, Inc. (Executive Producer). Linking Theory to Nursing Practice. Programs 5 & 6: Theory into Practice, 2005. [Instructional DVD]. (Available from Walden University, 155 5th Avenue South, Minneapolis, MN 55401).

5. M. E. Parker, *Nursing Theories and Nursing Practice* (Philadelphia: FA. Davis Company, 2001), 392-93.

6. *Family Consecration Prayer Book* (Kenosha, WI: St. Joseph Center, 1986), 20.

7. D. Johnson, "Development of Theory: A Requisite for Nursing as a Primary Health Profession," *Nursing Research,* 23(5), 372-377 (1974).

8. Ibid.

9. A. Boykin (Speaker). Laureate Education, Inc. (Executive Producer). Linking Theory to Nursing Practice. Programs 5 & 6: Theory into Practice, 2005. [Instructional DVD]. (Available from Walden University, 155 5th Avenue South, Minneapolis, MN 55401).

10. Ibid.

11. C. Cara, "Continuing Education: A Pragmatic View of Jean Watson's Caring Theory", *International Journal for Human Caring,* 7, 51-61 (2003). Retrieved September 24, 2007 from http://www2.uchsc.edu/son/caring/content/CaritasPractice.asp.

12. L. McDonald, *Florence Nightingale: Her Spiritual Journey* (2002). Retrieved September 24, 2007 from http://www.sociology.uoguelph.ca/fnightingale/.

13. C. Cara, "Continuing Education: A Pragmatic View of Jean Watson's Caring Theory", *International Journal for Human Caring,* 7, 51-61 (2003). Retrieved September 24, 2007 from http://www2.uchsc.edu/son/caring/content/CaritasPractice.asp.

14. "Health Care as God's Work", *Niagara Anglican*, 10, 15 (1999). Retrieved September 24, 2007 from http://www.sociology.uoguelph.ca/fnightingale/.

15. C. Cara, "Continuing Education: A Pragmatic View of Jean Watson's Caring Theory", *International Journal for Human Caring,* 7, 51-61 (2003). Retrieved September 24, 2007 from http://www2.uchsc.edu/son/caring/content/CaritasPractice.asp.

16. "Health Care as God's Work", *Niagara Anglican*, 10, 15 (1999). Retrieved September 24, 2007 from http://www.sociology.uoguelph.ca/fnightingale/.

17. C. Cara, "Continuing Education: A Pragmatic view of Jean Watson's Caring Theory", *International Journal for Human Caring*, 7, 51-61 (2003). Retrieved September 24, 2007 from http://www2.uchsc.edu/son/caring/content/CaritasPractice.asp.

18. F. Nightingale, *Letter to Sir Harry Verney*, (1890). Retrieved September 24, 2007 from http://www.sociology.uoguelph.ca/fnightingale/.

19. F. Nightingale, *Letter to Hilary Bonham Carter* (1846). Retrieved September 24, 2007 from http://www.sociology.uoguelph.ca/fnightingale/.

20. F. Nightingale, *Letter to Parthenope Verney* (1885). Retrieved September 24, 2007 from http://www.sociology.uoguelph.ca/fnightingale/.

21. L. McDonald, *Florence Nightingale: Faith and Work.* (2005). Retrieved September 24, 2007 from http://www.sociology.uoguelph.ca/fnightingale/.

22. C. Cara, "Continuing Education: A Pragmatic View of Jean Watson's Caring Theory", *International Journal for Human Caring*, 7, 51-61 (2003). Retrieved September 24, 2007 from http://www2.uchsc.edu/son/caring/content/CaritasPractice.asp.

23. "Health Care as God's Work", *Niagara Anglican*, 10, 15 (1999). Retrieved September 24, 2007 from http://www.sociology.uoguelph.ca/fnightingale/.

24. F. Nightingale, *Letter to Sir Harry Verney* (1890). Retrieved September 24, 2007 from http://www.sociology.uoguelph.ca/fnightingale/.

25. B. P. Houser and K. N. Player, *Pivotal Moments in Nursing: Leaders Who Changed the Path of a Profession* (Indianapolis, IN: Sigma Theta Tau International, 2004), 170.

Chapter 4

1. M. A. Burkhardt and A. K. Nathaniel, *Ethics & Issues in Contemporary Nursing* (2nd ed.) (Albany, NY: Delmar, 2002), 386.

2. B. Phillips and M. Reagan, *The All-American Quote Book* (Eugene, OR: Harvest House, 1995), 63.

3. M. E. Parker, *Nursing Theories and Nursing Practice* (Philadelphia: F. A. Davis Company, 2001), 6.

4. Ibid., 228-30.

5. M. Lloyd-Williams & S. Shah, "End of Life Decision Making- Have we Got It Right?" *European Journal of Cancer Care,* 12, 212-214 (2003).

6. J. Ufema, "Insights on Death and Dieing," *Nursing 2005,* 35, 74-75 (2005).

7. K. Kolsky, *End of Life: Helping With Comfort and Care* (Bethesda, MD: NIH, 2008), 17.

8. M. E. Parker, *Nursing Theories and Nursing Practice* (Philadelphia: F. A. Davis Company, 2001), 362.

9. Ibid., 362-65.

10. Ibid., 228-30.

11. Ibid., 228-31.

12. P. L. Chinn and M. K. Kramer, *Integrated Knowledge Development in Nursing*, (St. Louis, MI: Mosby, 2004), 45.

13. T. Burke, *Forbidden Grief: The Unspoken Grief of Abortion* (Springfield, IL: Acorn Books, 2002), 108-09.

14. Ibid., 32.

Chapter 5

1. M. E. Parker, *Nursing Theories and Nursing Practice* (Philadelphia: F. A. Davis Company, 2001), 32-50.

2. Ibid., 40-50.

3. J. Shovein, C. Huston, S. Fox, and B. Damazo "Challenging Traditional Teaching and Learning Paradigms: Online Learning and Emancipatory Teaching," *Nursing Education Perspectives, 26*(6), 340–343 (2005).

4. D. M. Billings and J. A. Halstead, *Teaching in Nursing: A Guide for Faculty* (2nd ed.) (St. Louis, MO: Elsevier Saunders 2005), 116.

5. M. Brady, "The Challenges of Technology," *Journal of Nursing Education*, 43, 4 (2004). Retrieved July 30, 2007 from http://ebsco.waldenu.edu/ehost/pdf?vid=6&hid=105&sid=0484b041-9ed4-415b-a63c-9d27ed7970d8%40session mgr107

Chapter 6

1. United States Department of Health and Human Services, *Privacy Rule Summary*, (2003). Retrieved July 25, 2008 from http://www.hhs.gov/ocr/hipaa/

2. M. E. Parker, *Nursing Theories and Nursing Practice* (Philadelphia: F. A. Davis Company, 2001), 172-77.

3. F. C. Biley, "Some Determinants that Effect Patient Participation in Decision-making About Nursing Care," *Journal of Advanced Nursing*, 17, 414-421 (2001).

4. M. E. Parker, *Nursing Theories and Nursing Practice* (Philadelphia: F. A. Davis Company, 2001), 174.

5. P. A. Reagan, and J. Brookins-Fisher, *Community Health in the 21st Century* (2nded.) (San Francisco: Benjamin Cummings, 2002), 269.

6. T. Knable, "Why are Baby Boomers Returning to College?" (2006). Retrieved March 25, 2006 from http://adulted.about.com/cs/studiesstats1/a/boomers.htm

7. Alzheimer Association, "2008 Alzheimer Disease Facts and Figures," *Alzheimer's and Dementia*, 4 (2) (2008). Retrieved July 25, 2008 from http://www.alz.org/national/documents/report_alzfactsfigures2008.pdf

8. P. A. Reagan, and J. Brookins-Fisher, *Community Health in the 21st Century* (2nded.) (San Francisco: Benjamin Cummings, 2002), 268-87.

9. Benedict XVI, "You are Christ's Disciples Today" (Speech from Yonkers, NY) *The Catholic Standard*, 58 (21), 24 (2008).

10. Webster's New World College Dictionary, (4th Ed.) (Foster City, CA: IDG Books Worldwide, Inc., 2001), 128.

11. P. A. Reagan, and J. Brookins-Fisher, *Community Health in the 21st Century* (2nded.) (San Francisco: Benjamin Cummings, 2002) 268-87.

12. Ibid.

Chapter 7

1. American Association of Colleges of Nursing. *AACN Position Statement on Defining Scholarship for the Discipline of Nursing*. Washington, DC: Author (1999). Retrieved July 2, 2007 from http://www.aacn.nche.edu/Publications/positions/scholar.htm

2. D. M. Billings, and J. A. Halstead, *Teaching in Nursing: A Guide for Faculty* (2nd Ed.) (St. Louis, MO: Elsevier Saunders, 2005), 287.

3. Ibid., 242, 297-298.

4. M. Weimer, *Learner-Centered Teaching* (San Francisco: Jossey-Bass, 2002), 12, 14.

5. M. Brain, *Emphasis on Teaching,* (1997) Retrieved August 3, 2007 from http://www.bygpub.com/eot/eot1.htm

6. Center for Advancement of Teaching and Learning, *Characteristics of the Superior College Teacher,* (n.d). Retrieved November 19, 2005 from http://www.k-state.edu/catl.htm

7. M. Brain, *Emphasis on Teaching,* (1997) Retrieved August 3, 2007 from http://www.bygpub.com/eot/eot1.htm

8. Center for Advancement of Teaching and Learning, *Characteristics of the Superior College Teacher,* (n.d.) Retrieved November 19, 2005 from http://www.k-state.edu/catl.htm

9. M. E. Parker, *Nursing Theories and Nursing Practice* (Philadelphia: F. A. Davis Company, 2001), 344-45.

10. D. M. Billings, and J. A. Halstead, *Teaching in Nursing: A Guide for Faculty* (2nd Ed.) (St. Louis, MO: Elsevier Saunders, 2005), 285-88.

11. M. Weimer, *Learner-Centered Teaching* (San Francisco: Jossey-Bass, 2002), 12, 14, 28-31.

12. D. M. Billings, and J. A. Halstead, *Teaching in Nursing: A Guide for Faculty* (2nd Ed.) (St. Louis, MO: Elsevier Saunders, 2005), 286-88.

Chapter 8

1. S. C. Grossman and T. M. Valiga, *The New Leadership Challenge: Creating the Future of Nursing* (Philadelphia: F. A. Davis Company, 2000), 47-48.

2. S. B. Bastable, *Nurses as Educator* (2nd Ed.) (Boston: Jones and Bartlett Publishers, 2003), 59.

3. R. Paul and R. Schriven, "Defining Critical Thinking", *The Critical Thinking Community,* The National Council for Excellence in Critical Thinking Instruction. Retrieved May 2, 2005 from http://www.criticalthinking.org/aboutCT/definingCT.shtml

4. "Critical Thinking: To Think like a Nurse". Retrieved May 2, 2005 from http://www.cariboo.bc.ca./nursing/faculty/heaslip/nrsct.htm.

5. Ibid.

6. S. C. Grossman and T. M. Valiga, *The New Leadership Challenge: Creating the Future of Nursing* (Philadelphia: F. A. Davis Company, 2000), 142-144.

7. Ibid.

Chapter 9

1 M. A. Burkhardt and A. K. Nathaniel, *Ethics & Issues in Contemporary Nursing* (2nd ed.) (Albany, NY: Delmar, 2002), 100-05.

2. B. Phillips and M. Reagan, *The All-American Quote Book* (Eugene, OR: Harvest House, 1995), 261.

3. Webster's New World College Dictionary, (4th Ed.) (Foster City, CA: IDG Books Worldwide, Inc., 2001) 297, 517.

4. Benedict XVI, "You are Christ's Disciples Today" (Speech from Yonkers, NY) *The Catholic Standard*, 58 (21), 24 (2008).

5. M. A. Burkhardt and A. K. Nathaniel, *Ethics & Issues in Contemporary Nursing* (2nd ed.) (Albany, NY: Delmar, 2002) 396.

6. D. J. Mason, J.K. Leavitt, and M.W. Chaffee, *Policy & Politics in Nursing and Health Care* (St. Louis: Saunders, 2002), 601.

7. Ibid., 610.

8. D. M. Billings and J. A. Halstead, *Teaching in Nursing: A Guide for Faculty* (2nd ed.) (St. Louis, MO: Elsevier Saunders 2005), 111-13.

9. S. Whittaker, W. Carson, and M.C. Smolenski, "Assuring Continued Competence: Policy Questions and Approaches: How Should the Profession Respond?" (2000) Retrieved on August 5, 2007 from http://nursingworld. org/ojin/topic10/tpc10_4.htm

10. N. Stanford-Blair (Speaker). Cantor & Associates. (Producer) The Nurse Leader: New Perspectives on the Profession. Program 5: Mindful Leadership, 2004. [Instructional DVD]. (Available from Walden University, 155 5th Avenue South, Minneapolis, MN 55401).

Chapter 10

1. M. R. Bleich, C. Connolly, K. Davis, B. Hatcher, P. O'Neall Hewlett and K. Stockley Hill, *Wisdom at Work: The Importance of the Older and Experienced Nurse in the Workplace* (Princeton, NJ: Robert Wood Johnson Foundation, 2006), 5.

2. Ibid., 8.

3. Ibid., 16.

4. Ibid., 22-23.

5. Ibid., 20.

6. Ibid., 27.

7. Ibid., 28.

8. Ibid., 30.

9. Ibid., 51-52.

10. Ibid., 51-52.

11. Ibid., 53.

Chapter 11

1. B. Phillips and M. Reagan, *The All-American Quote Book* (Eugene, OR: Harvest House, 1995), 130.

2. Ibid., 46.

3. Ibid., 73.

4. N. Stanford-Blair (Speaker). Cantor & Associates. (Producer) The Nurse Leader: New Perspectives on the Profession. Program 5: Mindful Leadership, 2004. [Instructional DVD]. (Available from Walden University, 155 5th Avenue South, Minneapolis, MN 55401).

5. K. Kerfoot (Speaker). Cantor & Associates. (Producer). The Nurse Leader: New Perspectives on the Profession. Program 6: Leadership in Practice, 2004. [Instructional DVD]. (Available from Walden University, 155 5th Avenue South, Minneapolis, MN 55401).

6. S. C. Grossman and T. M. Valiga, *The New Leadership Challenge: Creating the Future of Nursing* (Philadelphia: F. A. Davis Company, 2000), 17, 199-203.

7. E. M. Kopp and J. L. Hinkle "Understanding Mentoring Relationships," *Journal of Neuroscience Nursing, 38*(2), 126–131, (2006).

8. B. Phillips and M. Reagan, *The All-American Quote Book* (Eugene, OR: Harvest House, 1995), 100.

9. Benedict XVI, "You are Christ's Disciples Today" (Speech from Yonkers, NY) *The Catholic Standard*, 58 (21), 24 (2008).

10. K. Kerfoot (Speaker). Cantor & Associates. (Producer). The Nurse Leader: New Perspectives on the Profession. Program 6: Leadership in Practice, 2004. [Instructional DVD]. (Available from Walden University, 155 5th Avenue South, Minneapolis, MN 55401).

11. B. Phillips and M. Reagan, *The All-American Quote Book* (Eugene, OR: Harvest House, 1995), 32.

Breinigsville, PA USA
17 June 2010

240091BV00001B/19/P